# STILL RIDING AT 80

with profiles of twenty elder riders and drivers

# *Still Riding at* 8Ø

WITH *Profiles of Twenty Elder Riders and Drivers*

**HELEN HILLS**

Haley's
Athol, Massachusetts

International Standard Book Number:     978-1-884540-49-3
Library of Congress Control Number:     2010939035


Cover design by Michael Ruocco.


With thanks to the twenty elder horse people who have generously allowed the use of their photographs in this book



**Acknowledgments**
Marcia Gagliardi for being enthusiastic about the manuscript, Christel Sexton for providing relevant *Equus* articles, Althea Bramhall for helping me understand driving options, and Diane Godek, along with many other horse people, for directing me to elder riders and drivers




Haley's
488 South Main Street
Athol, Massachusetts 01331
800.215.8805
haley.antique@verizon.net

*To Jean McCurdy, Barbara Eriksson, Frank Thoma,*
*Ann Kendall, Linda Styles, Alan Berman, and David Bruce,*
*helpers and friends all, who have made it possible for me to*
*continue riding and caring for my horses*

*And in a special way to Susie Feldman,*
*who helped see me through horseless and other hard times*

# Contents

Preface . . . . . . . . . . . . . . . . . . . . . . . . . . . . . . . . . . . . . . . . . . . . . . xiii

**Part I: To Ride or Not to Ride**

Introduction. . . . . . . . . . . . . . . . . . . . . . . . . . . . . . . . . . . . . . . . . 3

Aging as It Affects Riding. . . . . . . . . . . . . . . . . . . . . . . . . . . . 7

    Expectations. . . . . . . . . . . . . . . . . . . . . . . . . . . . . . . . . . . . . . 7

    Physical concerns . . . . . . . . . . . . . . . . . . . . . . . . . . . . . . . . 9

    Mental concerns . . . . . . . . . . . . . . . . . . . . . . . . . . . . . . . . 13

Compensating for Aging Problems . . . . . . . . . . . . . . . . . . . 18

    Equipment . . . . . . . . . . . . . . . . . . . . . . . . . . . . . . . . . . . . . 18

    Strategies for safety and comfort. . . . . . . . . . . . . . . . . . 24

    Strategies for peace of mind . . . . . . . . . . . . . . . . . . . . . 32

    Practical matters . . . . . . . . . . . . . . . . . . . . . . . . . . . . . . . 35

Discovering What Lasts . . . . . . . . . . . . . . . . . . . . . . . . . . . . . 39

    Riding horses . . . . . . . . . . . . . . . . . . . . . . . . . . . . . . . . . . 39

    Caring for horses. . . . . . . . . . . . . . . . . . . . . . . . . . . . . . . 42

    Delighting in horses . . . . . . . . . . . . . . . . . . . . . . . . . . . . 44

Quitting Time. . . . . . . . . . . . . . . . . . . . . . . . . . . . . . . . . . . . . 46

    Without regrets. . . . . . . . . . . . . . . . . . . . . . . . . . . . . . . . 46

    Deciding . . . . . . . . . . . . . . . . . . . . . . . . . . . . . . . . . . . . . . 46

    After quitting. . . . . . . . . . . . . . . . . . . . . . . . . . . . . . . . . . 52

contents continued on the next page

## Part II: Twenty Celebratory Sketches

Presenting the Twenty . . . . . . . . . . . . . . . . . . . . . . . . . . . . . 61

Dan and Carol Rice . . . . . . . . . . . . . . . . . . 65

Alyse Aubin . . . . . . . . . . . . . . 73

Donald Grypko . . . . . . . . . . . . . . . . . . . . . 81

Judy Voll . . . . . . . . . . . . . . . . . . . . . . . . 87

Leonard "Whitey" Streeter . . . . . . . . . . . . . 95

Sue Hellen . . . . . . . . . . . . . . . . . . . . . . . . . . . . . . . . 101

Bill Kingman . . . . . . . . . . . . . . . . . . . . 107

Beverly Murphy . . . . . . . . . . . . . . . . . . . . . . . . . . 115

Marcy Gamester . . . . . . . . . . . . . . . . . . . . . . . . . 121

Dorothy McFarland . . . . . . . . . . . . . . . . . . . 129

Molly Scott . . . . . . . . . . . . . . . . . . . . . . . . 135

contents continued on the next page

Roberta Bryant . . . . . . . . . . . . . . . . . . . . . .143

Judy Smith . . . . . . . . . . . . . . . . . . . .149

Beth Jenkins. . . . . . . . . . . . . . . . . . . . . . . . . .157

Sy Cote . . . . . . . . . . . . . . . . . . . . . . . . . . . .165

Pat Kane. . . . . . . . . . . . . . . . . . . . . . . . . . .173

Polly Bartlett. . . . . . . . . . . . . . . . . . . . . . .179

Lyn Howard . . . . . . . . . . . . . . . . . . . . . . . . . 185

Nona King. . . . . . . . . . . . . . . . . . . . . . . . 191

Don Roberts . . . . . . . . . . . . . . . . . . . . . . 199

Afterword . . . . . . . . . . . . . . . . . . . . . . . . . . . . . . . 205

After Afterword. . . . . . . . . . . . . . . . . . . . . . . . . . . 207

Glossary of Equestrian Terms. . . . . . . . . . . . . . . . . 209

About the Author . . . . . . . . . . . . . . . . . . . . . . . . . 213

# Preface

I had just returned from a little slice of heaven. Of course I was on horseback, and an October sun was shining. My friend and I were riding through an extended bower of yellow and green leaves, with those soft russet ones whispering beneath us. I was being lulled by the back and forth, cradle-like movement of my horse beneath me. I wanted these moments to last forever.

I became eighty years old in December 2009. How many years of riding remain for me?

On this particular day, Jean and I were riding in a heavily wooded area off Gale Road in Warwick, Massachusetts, six miles from my home. Jean had connected my trailer to my truck, driven us up the steep road to our entry point, tacked up both horses, and then held my horse as I mounted. She had done all the work, because my shoulders and back are, to put it gently, fragile. And today she had Lulu as her mount, so I had the relaxing Lucky. We alternate the horses between us.

Lucky is a Quarter Horse mix, a dream trail horse, 15.1 hands, twenty-three years old, quiet, goes through anything, responsive, great gaits. Lulu is a Norwegian Fjord, 14.1 hands, fifteen years old, quiet, also goes through anything, with smooth gaits, but she can give a really big shy on occasion. She is responsive if she wishes and you insist, but her mind is basically occupied with one thing—eating. This can be very annoying when green branches are nose-close, as they were today. But I had been on Lucky and very happy all the way.

The night before, I had been uncomfortably tense about my upcoming ride. I always am in recent years, both the night and morning before. Am I nuts? I want to ride forever. I always eagerly schedule my next ride with Jean almost before we dismount.

A week or so before the Gale Road ride, we had ridden in the Lake Dennison area, about twenty miles from home. This was another A+ experience, only to be topped by the Gale Road one, probably because more recent. Not that every ride is a bit of heaven. Sometimes one of the horses is tired and drags, sometimes we come upon a scary situation, and weather not just right makes a difference also. But I always am wanting to know when I will next have the opportunity to mount and ride out.

It is on the night before a ride, and often between rides, that I wonder to myself: Should I stop riding? I am eighty years old. Are there reasons to quit? Actually, I suspect that I may be half looking for an excuse to stop, that is, until I am once again in the saddle, when I feel like a queen. Is my in-between angst a matter of age? A general loss of confidence is not unusual with age. Is it a fear for the safety of my aging body and the preservation of my life? If so, why now, when those concerns should have more appropriately been in my mind when I had four young children and nevertheless galloped exuberantly through the woods following hounds and a venturesome fox?

Thoughts such as these have made me look to the experience of other riders. I wonder why and when riders stop riding. What are their reasons? Are they always sorry or are they sometimes (perhaps secretly) glad to quit? What wisdom can be gleaned from them? Perhaps some have stopped needlessly, not realizing that they might have continued if they had known of the various strategies possible for continuing their sport.

Further, when do riders begin to think about stopping riding? I suspect that the idea occurs to them in their early sixties. At the age of sixty most people at least begin to suspect that they are getting old and start looking ahead toward their old age in a way they never did before. Often they are reminded by a hip that just won't allow them to mount easily or a knee that requires dropping a stirrup to relieve the pain after an hour out. This book may help sixtyish riders consider ways to ride longer. It may also reassure returning riders (primarily women in their middle years who rode as children and now have the opportunity to return to horses) that, with any luck, they may look forward to riding, not just for a few years, but into their seventies and perhaps eighties.

The first part of this book discusses how aging affects our riding, suggests techniques people have used or are using to continue, explores how they feel or felt about quitting, and looks into ways to ease the emptiness of no longer riding. The second part of the book tells stories, one by one, of twenty men and women seventy years of age and up, both those who continue and those who have recently stopped riding and driving, and how they deal with (or have dealt with) the question of when to stop. For convenience and because most drivers began as riders, I often use the word riders to include drivers as well.

For horse people—those of us with a real passion for horses—no longer riding or driving is a haunting eventuality. Let us begin to face it now, planning to push it as many years down the road as we can. There are ways, as you will see.

# Part I

## To Ride or Not to Ride?

# Introduction

Derived in part from stories about twenty elder riders and drivers, this book discusses concerns and strategies for riders and drivers approaching and beyond the age of seventy. It is written for and about mostly non-professional horse people who are passionate about horses. We are myriad, particularly in middle and western Massachusetts. We love our horses, care for them ourselves if we possibly can, and watch the weather closely each day to see if it will be a riding day. Much of our shopping for our horses is done at local stores, and we account for a large proportion of the sales. Most of us read equestrian magazines, watch television shows about horses, and belong to one or more equestrian associations. Sometimes we consult professional trainers, but often as not we figure out what to feed our horses, how to care for them, and how to improve our riding and driving skills by exchanging information with our equestrian friends.

I am one of you. A quick sketch is in order, so you know where I am coming from, and—just as importantly—where I am not coming from. I was born in 1929 in Pennsylvania, graduated from Wellesley College, married, moved to the Washington, D.C. area, and raised four children. As they left home, I became an editor/writer/administrator for the U.S. Department of Education. Almost twenty years ago I remarried, and my husband and I moved to Massachusetts with two horses, three dogs, and one cat to a four-acre property in the village of Warwick. I soon began and still continue to work part-time as a volunteer for elderly shut-ins with Franklin County Home Care Corporation.

A few years after moving to Massachusetts, I began writing my first book, *Aging Well: Exploring the Land of Our Later Years*. Two books of essays about finding joy in everyday life followed, and then came *Spiritual Living: What Matters and What Doesn't*. The titles tell you half of my qualifications to write this book—I am well acquainted with what happens as people age, and my focus is on living deeply and enjoying it.

The other half of my qualifications consists of my particular riding background. Although always in love with horses, I did not really start to ride until the age of thirty-four, when I joined a class of women learning traditional English riding, including jumping. After a few years, I began riding with a private fox hunt and exploring trails with a friend on weekends. My two horses were stabled at various places in the Maryland area. Only when I arrived in Massachusetts, at the age of sixty-two, did I begin caring for my own horses, which I continue to do. During this time, I have been riding trails near our property and trailering to other locations as well. While I occasionally pick up pointers about horses from books, magazines, and TV programs, I have never shown any horses, never consulted a horse trainer, never taken dressage lessons, never driven a horse, and only rarely entered endurance or competitive trail events. Because I greatly enjoy an uphill gallop or two interspersed with interesting conversation, I prefer to ride the trails with just one person rather than a group.

While I would call myself a competent rider, I am no expert on horse behavior and am certainly not writing as a professional. Nevertheless, I have my own light-hearted theories about riding that have worked pretty well so far. I speculate that, when someone new to an experienced horse puts her foot in the stirrup, the horse glances back with a weary and world-wise eye and asks himself three questions: "Who will be boss? Does she know my language? How uncomfortable will this be?" When on horseback, I toss out of my mind all the minutiae of equestrian booklearning and keep in mind only two basic facts from which all further training seems to emanate: Horses will move away from pressure, and they will try to retain their balance. This perhaps simplistic approach works well, of course, only when riding horses with basic training. Beyond those two facts, I rely on my own experience, a conversational empathy with animals of various sorts, and common sense. Particularly the last.

Now for a few comments about practical matters. At the end of the book is a glossary of terms that might be puzzling to a non-equestrian reader of this book. The definitions are short and sweet, merely enough to make the surrounding text understandable to the general reader.

As for word usage, I refer to people of seventy years of age not as the "elderly," but as "elders," to suggest the wisdom that may come with age. "Elderly," as currently used in the United States, does not properly describe the people in my sketches. They are not only hearty but vibrant when we talk about horses and riding.

When writing about non-specific horsepeople and horses in the singular, I have chosen to refer to people as feminine and horses as masculine.

A final practical note is that all towns and cities mentioned are in Massachusetts unless otherwise stated.

Author profits from sales of this book will be donated to the New England Land Management Conservation Corporation (NEELMCC), which manages the New England Equestrian Center of Athol (NEECA), for further development of the facilities at its equestrian park.

# Aging as It Affects Riding

## Expectations

"Turning fifty, sixty, or even seventy certainly doesn't have to mean giving up your favorite sport. Riding can be good for you, no matter how old you are," blithely states an article in the March 2005 issue of *Equus* magazine, encouragingly titled "Never Too Old to Ride." Riders in their fifties were consulted on how their aging affected their riding. In their fifties? Young whippersnappers, some riders in their seventies and eighties would say. And so would I.

The same article, by Lee Farren, reports that riders over fifty years of age comprise about a quarter of actively competing members of the U.S. Dressage Federation, a third of the American Endurance Ride Conference, and two-thirds of the National Senior Pro Rodeo Association.

That people are living longer and leading more active lives is increasingly obvious. A *New York Times* article (January 8, 2010) by Kirk Johnson recounts stories about the increasing number of athletic adventures of people over eighty years of age. It reported that "at a Boston-based company that specializes in older travelers, adventure tours have gone from sixteen percent of passenger volume in 2001 to fifty percent for advance bookings this year." A similar rise in adventure-tour options has occurred in Exploritas (previously known as Elderhostel). One of the stories in the article recounted the putdown a lady received at base camp in a group heading for the South Pole. She was boasting about being eighty and was informed that three in the group were older than she.

Stories of people riding well into their eighties and beyond are not hard to find. These people are written about, of course, both because there have not been that many of them and also because most of us have not yet adjusted to the emerging fact that more people these days remain physically fit much longer than their parents and certainly their grandparents.

I found the following three stories in *Equus*, which graciously ran a search for me of its prior issues for articles on the subject. The first tells about ninety-three-year-old Miss Emily Ravenel Farrow of Charleston, South Carolina, a prominent riding instructor in Charleston during the 1930s and 1940s, who gave an interview in early 2009 to Julia Drake, also a horsewoman. In a moving article, Drake recounts her interview with "Miss Em," who told her of a wonderful experience on her most recent birthday. Referring to her retired American Saddlebred, Scamp, she said: "My friends took me over to Black Bottom Farm where he is boarded. It took three people to get me up on him. But I got up on him! My back straightened. My heels went down and my hands just went into place. It felt like home. I was home." The author said that Miss Em ended by saying that she hopes to ride him again on every succeeding birthday.

And then there was Connie Douglas Reeves, at the time the oldest living honoree of the National Cowgirl Museum's Hall of Fame. She was a riding instructor for many years at Camp Waldemar in Hunt, Texas, and died at the age of 101 when she was thrown from her favorite horse and fractured a vertebra in her neck. She had ridden nearly every day until then but had stopped teaching a few years before because of failing eyesight and hearing. In her nineties, she wrote her memoir, *I Married a Cowboy*, about her earlier life with her husband, raising sheep and cattle as well as caring for horses at the camp. She said that there are "five things essential to teach young riders: confidence, relaxation, rhythm, balance and common sense." (Frankly, I am not sure that horseback riding at the age of 101 showed much common sense.)

Finally there is Beryl Grilley, who in March 2005 was ninety-four years old and still riding out into the Oregon mountains, often by herself at sunset. She is quoted in an article by Lee Farrenas as giving this advice to those who want to keep riding: "Just ride. That's the best advice I can give."

Considering all these examples of very elder people engaged in physically demanding adventures, we can be inspired. With any luck, we elders may have more than a few rides ahead of us.

## Physical concerns

Even enthusiastic, competent, and dedicated riders may experience a serious illness in their middle years that makes being on a horse uncomfortable, unsafe, or downright impossible. That is tough stuff, because riding provides special pleasures for those of us fortunate enough to retain good health past seventy years of age. For us, it is the slow process of aging that gradually accomplishes the inevitable, and we find that we must—or ought to—hang up our stirrups.

It is inescapable as the years go by that we will experience unwelcome changes in bones, tendons, joints, and muscles. Over my years of riding with other people, usually younger than I, the complaint I have heard most often concerns pain in the knees. Toward the end of a ride, at a leisurely walk home, they will kick off their stirrups "to rest my knees." Or perhaps a left knee will inhibit mounting or make it, at the least, uncomfortable.

If not a knee or two, aging hips and back need relief from the swinging and swaying of a walk or the unevenness of a rough trot. I haven't the knee problem, but I do know the pleasure, after dismounting, of sitting on something that doesn't move at all. Our backs are not all that happy either about carrying heavy buckets of water for our horses to drink, not to mention moving bales of hay or bags of shavings.

Our shoulders, too, seem to be wearing out at a faster rate than they used to. Twenty years ago, I had never heard of rotator cuff surgery, but since then it has become quite common. Now I know about it only too well, because I have had rotator cuff surgery on both shoulders. I have been warned not to extend my arms into certain positions or lift much weight for fear that the rotator cuff on my right shoulder might just tear again, beyond repair by another operation. Those dreaded situations just happen to include raising my arm high enough to groom a tall horse, put a bridle on him, or lift a saddle onto his back. Fortunately, no harm occurs when exerting pressure on the reins to slow a horse as long as my arms are by my side—as of course they should be anyway.

We do not help the muscles and joints in our knees, backs, and shoulders, either, by raking up manure from stalls and fields, lifting it into a wheelbarrow, pushing that increasingly heavy wheelbarrow to wherever it has to go, and putting it on edge to dump the manure. And who has a horse that isn't liberal with manure, night and day, winter and summer?

Age invariably brings with it pains in our joints, simple osteoarthritis if we are lucky. This finger, that toe, certainly part of the back, sometimes the neck—no one over fifty seems to escape entirely. Those whose lives involve continual exercise perhaps are affected later, but I have been assured for years by one medical person after another that "everyone your age has some arthritis." For horse people that means less agility. We may creak a bit as we mount a horse or compensate less smoothly for an unexpected movement by the horse beneath us. We take a little longer to warm up to activities such as shoveling, raking, and carrying. Still, no big deal for the horse person. File it under "inconvenience."

A more annoying problem that creeps up on most of us as we get older is a decrease in balance, relevant to riders long before we notice a similar decrease in walking. I remember my surprise some years ago when I was about to run down a short but steep grassy hill. I was on the edge of flinging out my arms to the side and letting her rip when something inside me said, "No, you can't do this."

"What?" said I. "Of course I can. I always have."

But I didn't that time. The something inside me was correct. I simply no longer had the assured balance of my youth.

For the rider, balance can be an issue in mounting, even with the assistance of a mounting block. A year or so ago, as I was about to mount, I sensed in myself an uncertainty as to whether I could actually do it safely. I was standing high enough and I was mounting my short Norwegian Fjord. And yet the prospect of bouncing on the stirrup and swinging my other leg way over the broad saddle made me hesitate. We all know that at the second of mounting a horse we are quite vulnerable if he moves in an unexpected direction, leaving us with one foot perhaps caught in the left stirrup as we fall. We depend on our speed and balance. Of the latter I was surprised to discover I had become deficient.

Happily, balance while in the saddle is a different matter. Apparently, if we have ridden long and well enough, our by-now-automatic balance with the movement of the horse does not readily disappear. Nor have I noted slow reaction time in response to a shy. Once mounted on my horse, my balance and reflexes remain fine. Because one hears of the danger of slow reaction time for elderly drivers, I have been pleasantly surprised not to note this in myself when riding—or in driving a car, as a matter of fact. And none of the riders I have interviewed mentioned it as a concern.

A basic and universal physical problem for riders as they enter their later years is the gradual decrease in energy. In our youth, most of us had plenty of get-up-and-go all day long. In fact, I prided myself on being a person with high energy. Now I still have times when I feel only about forty years old and can't wait to do this and that, but I find that such periods are much shorter than they used to be and come much less frequently.

Because the change is gradual, many of us just ignore it and manage to enjoy our livelier moments. We riders hope such moments coincide with our riding, but that of course is not always so.

In our seventies, a four-hour trail ride in the most pleasant and easiest of circumstances seems just too long. Our bodies keep asking us the child's question, "How much farther, Mom?" Because most of us do not want to seem old with our usually younger companions, we keep quiet about feeling a little tired. For those of us who care for our horses at our homes, the ordinary barn tasks are harder and take longer. Not only must manure somehow disappear from our stalls and fields, but hay must be moved, loose shavings shoveled or packaged shavings carried and dumped, water buckets filled and carried, and bags of grain emptied into large rodent-safe containers. There is also the matter of a gradual decrease in muscle strength. Every year the weight of hay, shavings, grain, and water buckets seems to increase, so that whereas ten or so years ago we thought nothing of these tasks, now we dread them or arrange for someone else to do them.

Consider also the dark, cold, snowy, windy mornings when bed is so warm. Goodness, we are seventy-something years old. Don't we deserve a little rest on such a morning? Must we really pull ourselves out of bed, throw on all that clothing, push our tired feet into boots, and venture out? Yes, of course we must: we own horses. They are out there in the weather waiting for us. They have been standing there all the long night. They need hay to warm their guts and chase away the night's cold. They are waiting for us, looking for us, perhaps calling for us. So we drag ourselves out of bed and do what is necessary.

Once in the barn with the horses, the effort for most of us feels worth it. The neighing, the eager welcome, and the ever-amazing size and strength of these animals make us forget the effort it takes to force a seventy-something body to do one's

12

will. And for me, there is the special treat of being able to run my hand through the thick coat on Lulu's wide, fuzzy back and then snuggle into her warm muscular neck as I slip the halter over her head.

Even tacking up becomes more burdensome with the years. There is all that grooming of a back possibly above our shoulder level, bending over to lift and clean hooves, brushing the often dirt-encrusted coat, disentangling the mane and tail, and then—finally—bridling and saddling. All before we can even get to the pleasure part of riding. Or perhaps we begin to skip some of those steps—not really necessary steps, we say, something we can do later.

It was about ten years ago that I began to wish I were Queen Elizabeth, who, at least in my imagination, emerges from her palace in her spanking-clean riding apparel and without further ado mounts, graciously assisted by a groom, onto a horse brushed to sparkling sheen, tacked up, ready to go. In recent years, I have in effect become Queen Elizabeth when I emerge from my palace to ride, and my riding buddy performs the required steps. (Speaking of the Queen, in a why-not-nothing-to-lose spirit, I tried to contact her by letter, requesting a royal word about her current riding to insert in this book. Her staff replied with a most polite, "The Queen has made it a rule not to comment on such matters.")

So much for physical problems that discourage us from caring for and riding our horses. I will discuss below various strategies that may enable us to push time back a bit.

### Mental concerns

Partially because we are loath to acknowledge them, mental concerns can be more difficult to deal with than physical. Earliest to arrive is a failing memory. The first sign, occurring perhaps in our fifties, is that we hurriedly go downstairs because we have to—but what was it we came downstairs to do? After this memory lapse happens often enough, we just resignedly say, "Oh, yes," run back upstairs, and then somehow know that as we turn around to go back down, we will remember. We wanted to feed the dog.

Next comes forgetting everyone's name except our own, and sometimes we worry about that too. Losing names of course starts with people to whom we have just been introduced, moves to acquaintances, and sometimes includes even our good friends and their mates. All sorts of trick remedies are suggested in magazines and television shows, and some of them may help some people some of the time in some situations. They offer no permanent cure. File this problem under "nuisance" and ignore it.

Memory problems are an annoyance to horse people who care for their horses at home. Whereas a dog or cat is usually inside and will pester us at feeding time, a horse in a barn or field has no sure way of telling us we are forgetting him. He can neigh and run around, but unless we are within hearing and seeing distance, we cannot pick up his request. And then there are the myriad actions we must take each time we go to the barn, differing by how we run our stable. Always there are the hay and the water, sometimes the grain, and of course manure removal. As we leave, gates and doors must be closed, water and lights turned off. If one horse has to be tied up while the other eats, as in my barn with Lulu, then there is remembering to release her after the appropriate interval. In addition, we must not forget to buy and get the hay into the barn one way or another, do the worming on time, call the blacksmith at the appropriate interval, schedule the vet, and then remember to be on hand the days of the appointments.

A second change in the mental category, one that sneaks up on us, is a loss of confidence in ourselves as we age. I refer to a general decrease in confidence, not just in relation to riding horseback. It comes, I believe, from a subconscious knowledge that all or most of our faculties are becoming less efficient. Remember my surprise that I didn't feel safe about running gaily down a short hill? And that occurred at least ten years ago. If we are honest (and many of us are not, particularly in this respect), we are less confident about our ability to drive a car anywhere, in rain or snow, at dusk or night. We would actually prefer to let our son or daughter do the driving. And yet, when we actually do drive under difficult conditions, we do it very well. Our lack of confidence seems ungrounded, definitely premature.

I have noticed in myself as well as others that not wanting to do a particular thing often precedes by some considerable time actually not being able to. The not wanting seems to forecast the eventual inability. Our unconscious is sending us a message, a prediction of the not-so-distant future.

Decreasing faith in our own abilities seems to occur in many parts of our lives as the years increase. Often an older person who has always appeared sure of herself will for no apparent reason easily credit the other guy with superior knowledge or judgment. Even if her hearing and sight have remained excellent, she will wonder if she has missed something, if there has been some failure either in the information she has taken in or the way she has processed it. The friends I have in mind as I write this and in whom I have observed this behavior are clearly intelligent and functioning in all respects at a high level. Why in the world would they so easily accede to another's opinion so contrary to their own? Answer: they are experiencing the decrease in self-confidence endemic to aging. It is a change that we must first acknowledge and then consciously fight. And of course, at eighty years of age, I myself am fully engaged in that fight.

To ride well and with enjoyment, confidence is necessary. Lack of it in a rider is felt by the horse immediately, leading to all sorts of problems, from miscommunication to fearfulness and even to outright disobedience. A horse, by his very nature, wants to know who is the herd leader, who is boss. He is more at ease if his rider takes over the responsibility of their safety, but if she won't, then he must—which may lead to a shy that would not have occurred if his rider had not been apprehensive.

Many riders and handlers of horses, whatever their age, lack confidence in their ability to control horses. Trainers often write about this common problem. After all, we are dealing with a large and potentially dangerous animal, a prey animal whose way of seeing and reacting to the world differs widely from ours. For a large number of people, the struggle to increase their confidence as riders and handlers is a continuing one. And then with the passage of time a general decrease in confidence makes the struggle even more difficult. Discouraging, but true. We rarely acknowledge this effect of aging, because that can put us one step back in the fight. Pretending in this case can be a good thing.

A positive change, usually coming even before a decrease in confidence, is that we gradually become less daring. We have less nerve. We may be fully confident, but not daring, which goes way beyond, often into what is foolish. There is a feeling of exhilaration to it that appeals to youth. By middle age, often we know better than to go beyond what is reasonably safe; and by the seventies, unless we are bent on pretending to be younger than we are, we have no taste for unnecessarily risking our lives. We may be fully confident, but not daring.

I remember when I was fox hunting in my forties (which then seemed old to me in comparison to others in the hunt), I had no doubt that I could handle whatever came to me. I remember saying to myself, when faced with a higher fence than usual and watching another horse and rider clear it, "If he can do it, I can do it." This is, of course, not necessarily true. I usually rode a very athletic (but hot) mare, so I had complete faith in my mount's ability to negotiate whatever was put before her. And so she did, even once managing to complete a jump at an angle in order to avoid a child on a pony who suddenly appeared beside us at the apex of the coop.

I have noted in speaking with riders, primarily aged sixty and up, a third concern—an increasing fear of becoming injured, and so having to lean on a cane or spend the rest of life stuck in a wheelchair. We are aware that our bodies are more easily injured and less easily repaired. A fall that would cause little or no injury to a younger person might cause long-lasting or even permanent impairment to us.

When one thinks about it, a serious injury early in life could alter more years than an injury later in life, when we have already enjoyed years of health. It seems odd, in a way, that when we have already lived so much of our life, we should find the few remaining years more precious than the many years before us in our youth, years that were being risked by our daring deeds. Furthermore, when young, we often have children and others dependent on us, whereas in our later years this is usually not the case. Perhaps we have simply learned, through years of living, both how precarious life is and also how wonderful it can be. Several of the people I interviewed expressed this feeling.

## Compensating for Aging Problems

At last we have come to some solutions or partial solutions for the problems of aging as they affect riders. There are numerous ways to compensate. Most are just common sense, but not all of us may have thought of them ourselves. I have gleaned the suggestions from books, magazines, other riders, and my own experience. They relate first to equipment and then to strategies to combat both physical concerns and mental ones. They may increase not only safety and comfort but peace of mind as well and, as such, they are worth consideration.

### Equipment

Absolutely essential, and usually required in group events, is the riding helmet, certified by the ASTM / SEI (American Society for Testing and Materials / Safety Equipment Institute), properly fitted, and with the strap fastened. It has saved countless lives during falls. And let's face it. If you ride horseback with any regularity, you will fall sometime. It happens. Afterward, you remount, for a while you feel somewhat stunned, and for even longer you will feel less confident, but you will probably not have injured your most precious of body parts—your brain.

Another piece of equipment that protects body parts in case of a fall is a safety vest, alternately termed a "crash vest" or "body protector vest." Last summer I bought myself one after reading about them in an issue of *Horse Journal*, a monthly publication that rates equestrian supplies. (It resembles the more familiar *Consumer Reports.*) The purpose of the vest is to "cushion the blow from a blunt injury, such as hitting the ground or being kicked." It does not protect from all injuries of the upper torso but enough to make it worthwhile as a protection for the back and ribs. Safety vests are required for many sports, including the equestrian competitions of eventing and racing. They are available at various levels of certification. Most recently, some equestrian eventers have begun to wear inflatable air bag vests, which motorcyclists have been using for about ten years.

A proper fit at the time of purchase is essential. I spent some time adapting it to my sloping shoulders so as to make it as comfortable as possible. The first time I wore the safety vest, with the temperature outside near eighty degrees, I simply couldn't handle the heat and the strange feeling of constriction. I took it off. When I next tried it, the weather was cooler, and after about fifteen minutes I had forgotten I was wearing a vest. I have learned not to tighten it on myself until just before mounting—in fact, as my riding buddy was tightening the girth on my horse, I was tightening my own girth. And after dismounting and loosening my safety vest, I found that it fit very nicely over my left arm, same as a saddle. I plan to continue using the vest, just in case. I figure, why not?

*The author at 80 fully attired with helmet and safety vest (not yet zipped), about to set out on Lulu, her Norwegian Fjord*

Mounting blocks have become much more popular than they used to be, and they are worth their weight in gold. (Have you ever tried mounting a horse while standing on the hubcap of your trailer? I have, and I don't recommend it.) I remember being very proud in my sixties of being able to mount quickly unaided. I did not think about the possibility that the process might be a bit uncomfortable for the horse, since I was putting all my weight on the stirrup and perhaps pulling the saddle and his skin a bit to the left. Now I depend on a mounting block, and I suspect my horses are pleased. The increased comfort to the horse can serve as an excuse for using the block if we don't want to admit that mounting from the ground is not as easy as it used it be.

*After her riding buddy Jean McCurdy has saddled Lulu, the author prepares to mount with the help of a mounting block*

But what if we are out on the trail, dismount to move a branch blocking the path, and then we need to mount again?

I suspect most of us will just find a big rock or a fallen tree that we can coax our horse to move toward on the left. However, if no such thing presents itself, we need have no fear. There seems to be a multitude of gadgets that we might have had the forethought to purchase and have remembered to attach to our saddle or otherwise bring with us. The June 2004 *Equus* magazine mentions different types of stirrup extenders, which lower the stirrup by two to eight inches, some removable. I actually purchased one of these some years ago, packed it with me, and attempted to use it. After I had extended the stirrup far enough to get my toe firmly onto it, I did my bounce and discovered I was not high enough to get my right leg well over the horse to actually mount. A rather awkward situation, amusing to my buddy. The gadget now rests on a shelf in my barn. Then there is Giddy-Up, a ten-inch folding stool that can be hitched onto a saddle and that I guess pretends to be a mounting block—but not a very high one.

Once mounted, with our heels firmly pressed downward in the stirrups, it may be that our ankles resent this unnatural position and feel strained. For this problem, the same *Equus* article, concerned as much with comfort as safety, suggests special stirrup cushion pads "with grip strips" that not only keep the foot from slipping as do the hard rubber stirrup pads that most of us English riders use, but also "diminish the effect of concussion" when wrapped around a conventional stirrup pad and held in place with Velcro. And of course many types of stirrups are available for the English rider—hinged, jointed, swivel, wedged, and adjustable to a preset angle.

Now that we are up in the saddle, with our feet comfortably and properly in the stirrups, perhaps we worry that a long ride will tire our posterior. Never fear, there is equipment to meet that need. "Seat softeners" are available for both Western and English riders, with a choice of materials in the padding and the cover. Some saddles even come with padding built into the seat—unnecessary if we have already bought undergarments, breeches, or jeans specially padded for riding. Or perhaps some of us come sufficiently padded without any purchase.

We should at this point be ready to ride out in comfort, but no, perhaps our hands are arthritic and we need gloves with rubberized grip pads or a pimpled texture in order to have a firm grip on the reins. These may be bought laced, plaited, rubber-coated, and even equipped with leather "handstops at incremental points." The article did not discuss the various types of gear for our legs, merely mentioning half chaps that come in many styles as a substitute for traditional tall boots for the English-style rider. The only obvious omission in this article on "comforts" was the boot jack, of which I personally have four or five stowed here and there, not only to help me slip out of my tall (rubber) riding boots but to use with some of my other recalcitrant shoes and boots.

And then there are braces for our knees, ankles, necks, and backs sold in the local pharmacy. If we need more support than these elastic braces, the December 2009 *Equus* magazine informs us that many kinds are available, some with solid or semisolid sides.

Of course the most important contribution to comfort is a proper saddle, hopefully on a horse with smooth gaits. Choices are myriad, and I shall spare you a discussion of them here. Somehow or other, most riders seem to solve what seems to me a major problem, namely, fitting the upper surface of the saddle to their posteriors and the lower surface to their horse's back, all without taking the horse himself into the tack shop. Once that is solved, there is a matter of weight as we lift the saddle up and over. If lifting a heavy Western saddle onto the back of our horse makes us groan, or if even an English saddle seems to be getting heavier, we might consider a much lighter-weight synthetic saddle.

Wintec is the most familiar brand of synthetic, and the name is used in much the same way as we refer to all tissues as Kleenex. While I have never been as comfortable as I was in my old, heavy leather Steuben Siegfried, I do just fine in my Wintec saddles. I bought my first when my shoulders were just recovering from rotator cuff surgery, and I knew lifting the leather saddles would cause trouble. To make mounting easier, I replaced one of my tall (and not very obliging) horses with the delightfully short Norwegian Fjord mare and at that time decided to go one step further and buy a Wintec for her. Soon I bought another Wintec to fit my taller Quarter Horse. Amusingly, soon after acquiring the lightweight saddles, I took one further step toward protecting my shoulders and back by handing over the task of saddling both horses to my riding buddy.

If weight is not a problem and safety is a primary concern, an Australian saddle might be a good choice. Western saddles

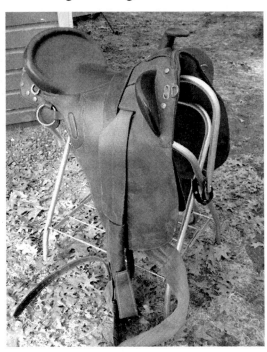

*The Australian leather saddle*
*recommended by Don Grypko*

have traditionally been considered not only more comfortable on a long ride, but also safer because of their deep seat and the horn. Website information from The Australian Stock Saddle Company describes the saddle as a "big dressage saddle," but it looks more like some sort of Western saddle. The website says that the stirrups hang in a dressage position and are free-swinging. Sometimes, but not always, they incorporate aspects of Western saddles, such as Western rigging, fleece-lined panels, fenders, and horns. The website explains why they are considered safer than other saddles for trail riding. I have synthetic saddles myself, and although I admire the beauty of the leather saddle, I cannot but think of all the work required to keep that intricate leather saddle in clean, supple, and pristine condition! Perhaps I am getting lazy as I age?

## Strategies for safety and comfort

By the time we reach seventy years of age, most of us are wise and clever enough to have devised various ways to compensate for the pains and annoyances of aging. This wisdom should include an acknowledgment that we simply cannot do everything we once did. We have to pull back and do a bit of scheming.

When we handle and ride horses, our most obvious source of danger and distress is the horse himself. This is no time to show off to our co-riders how well we can tame and train a hot, easily scared, unpredictable animal. Being dumped hurts more than it used to, and our muscles, joints, and bones require a lot longer to heal. Most horses have their quirks, and it may be that we and the horse we already own understand each other well enough to avoid dangerous nonsense. If not, there are many quiet, well-trained horses out there just waiting for a chance to work with us in the arena or to be our reliable trail companion. Such horses deserve a chance to share our lives more than do those with an attitude. Sometimes we need to switch horses, difficult as it can be to adjust to a new animal. We should consider leasing a horse to make sure it is reliable before we buy one or riding school horses at a nearby stable before we decide we are too old to ride safely anymore. (Approximate costs for group and individual riding lessons at local stables are given below.)

Then there is the matter of comfort. Although somehow or other I have never in my long life of riding ridden a gaited horse, I am assured by everyone who has that I have missed a distinct pleasure. I am sure that is true, having watched friends glide along smoothly on their gaited mounts while I posted or sat the trot on mine. I have simply never felt any discomfort on my various non-gaited horses, possibly because I have been lucky not to have chosen rough–gaited horses and not to have had knee or hip problems.

Next there is consideration of where we ride. Most of us ride trails at least occasionally, and I suspect that in Massachusetts, especially in the forested middle and western sections, we spend more of our mounted time on trails than in arenas. Hopefully, we are on a seasoned trail horse or following someone whose horse does not shy easily, is willing to cross water, and can settle down to a leisurely pace when asked. Although I have often ridden lead on a neophyte trail horse, I know that there is little reason (beyond pride) to force a horse to do something scary to him when there is an easier way—like following his buddy.

Many people dismiss trail riding as easy and relaxing, with the unstated assumption that anybody who can climb onto a horse can do it easily. We just put a friend on a companion horse behind us, explain that you pull back to stop, sit up straight, put down your heels, and off we go. Trail riding is often not considered a discipline or something for which we need basic riding skills, experience on horseback, and safety practices. And yet knowledge and experience, as well as a good basic seat, are mighty handy when we face various kinds of water crossings, steep hills, deep mud, and the scary unexpected. In group trail riding, the lack not only of experience but of widely understood rules often causes accidents and certainly discomfort and irritation to the more considerate and experienced trail riders who have to put up with inconsiderate novices. (I am resisting the temptation to list here "rules of the road" for trail riding.)

It is useless to remind horse owners that they should never ride alone, because deciding never to ride without a companion often severely limits the number of times we can ride. The weather does enough limiting, and it is tempting when the sun is shining just to saddle up quickly and take a short turn on the nearby path. Because of the unforeseen critters and other hazards in the woods and the scary nature of horses, riding alone is foolish. Luck is what keeps lone riders safe, and sometimes there isn't any at hand. Cell phones (where they work) help, as do notes left for friends or family, but neither provides the safety of a buddy. Always riding with a buddy is a rule I have finally learned to obey during the past ten years or so.

Another obvious strategy for minimizing discomfort and pain in the saddle is simply to ride shorter distances. We can decide not to participate in long group rides, particularly endurance and competitive rides, and we should alert possible companions ahead of time that an hour or two are all we want to be mounted.

Riding anywhere has its dangers, as we all know. However, riding in an arena limits those dangers, particularly if indoors at a stable. Other people are likely to be around to provide assistance if we need it. No deer will suddenly run across our path, the smell of bears will not put our horse on edge, and it is unlikely that a flock of birds will start up from the undergrowth. There will be noises but ones that our horse is used to if we ride regularly in a particular arena. Dressage is an intellectually and physically challenging arena sport, with the safety of an enclosed area, people about, and usually a trainer experienced with the vagaries of horses to provide help if needed. (Approximate local costs for dressage lessons are given below.)

Although in my thirties I thoroughly enjoyed group riding lessons in an arena, as did most of us who lived in suburbs, I now would find giving up the trail for the arena difficult. In an arena, we tend to concentrate on how well we and our horse are communicating—even without a teacher in the middle instructing us. Often riders use an arena solo, without a companion, to exercise and train themselves and their horse. The experience is more intellectual, more a lesson, without the relaxation and interesting terrain of the trails. That sounds like work to me, although I am well aware that many discover it to be very enjoyable. Most riders find the niche most suited to them.

A more interesting (at least to me) type of arena riding might be participating in a drill team, in which a group of riders works in unison "to create a dance on horseback," looking toward competitions and public performances. Drill team riding seems to be spreading, particularly among high school students. In Orange, the Crimson Acres drill teams under Sandy Whitmore are members of the United States Equestrian Drill Team Association and include beginner and novice teams as well as advanced and adult teams. There is safety in numbers here, pleasure in companionship, and pride in accomplishment. The only problem for someone over seventy might be the short-term memory required to execute the intricate patterns of the sport.

Some riders who experience certain types of physical pain when mounted or in the act of mounting switch to driving, because they find it more comfortable. Driving is certainly not safer than riding, in that an accident involves a cart in addition to horse and driver. Also, hitching a cart generally requires two people with some physical strength, and for elders no longer in their prime it can be taxing on various muscles and joints. All the aids of body position, balance, and touch, so familiar and relied upon by a rider, are of course mostly absent when we are sitting, not on the horse's back, but on a comfortable seat yards behind the horse. Clearly anyone starting to drive would do well to get professional help, because the skills it requires differ from those of riding.

Most drivers began as riders, some switching early in their lives to the sport. More people over fifty now seem to be showing interest in driving. In fact, most competitive drivers are in their fifties or sixties. At the World Singles Driving Competition in Italy in 2008, the average age of the competitors was sixty-two, and the winner was sixty-nine. Similarly, the best U.S. driving team members in the 2009 Poland competition were all in their sixties except one, and the best overall performance was given by a sixty-eight-year-old Dutch citizen. (Approximate local costs of carts, harness, and driving lessons are given below.)

A fairly new and increasingly popular variation to conventional driving of horses and ponies is the use of miniature horses, referred to as "minis." The cost of feed is considerably less, and these small animals—although with all the flight instincts of other horses—seem less frightening and easier to handle. For elders with shoulder and back problems, harnessing a mini would be ever so much easier than lifting the equipment up to horse- or even pony-level. Minis can easily pull an adult in a cart.

Whatever equestrian discipline or practice we decide to pursue—whether it be trail riding, equitation, dressage, driving, or cutting cattle—it helps to be physically fit. As we all know, physical fitness is "in." Articles abound on this subject, and equestrians are among those urged to do all sorts of exercises before and after riding. We are advised to develop a balanced fitness program, including sit-ups, leg lifts, and crunches and certainly stretching to warm up before riding. Much emphasis is given to learning to breathe properly before and while mounted.

(Breathing properly is basic to the currently popular Centered Riding movement.) I am sure all this is wise, but I suspect that most horse people, at least those who care for their own horses, get what feels like enough exercise just doing barn chores and are not eager for any more, particularly just before mounting. Perhaps I speak here only for my own increasingly indolent self!

Advice on how to do those barn chores is also available, most of it not new to those of us who have done it for years. Nevertheless, a listing of some of what are called "Back-Saving Techniques" by Susan Kauffman in the October 2009 *Equus* might serve as a reminder. Primary among the suggestions is using the legs rather than the back and bending the knees to lift a wheelbarrow rather than bending over with the back. We are also told not to load the wheelbarrow so high that it will be too heavy to push but to make extra trips despite the increase in time spent. Other suggestions include alternating chores, bending at the knees to lift heavy items (such as bales of hay, bags of grain, filled water buckets, saddles), and centering and balancing them when possible.

The almost universal problem that those of us over seventy face, rarely mentioned in relation to horses, has to do with that increasing daily nuisance of diminishing short-term memory noted above. If we are feeding our own horses, we must remember to do it—simple as that. However, if we are engaged in some fascinating task or preparing to go to some enchanting social event, it is possible that even feeding our beloved horses can slip our minds. This has not happened to me yet, but I sense that it could, and so I have taken several steps to prevent it that might prove adaptable to others' situations.

First of all, I see my day as divided into three parts, each beginning at a very specific time with the morning feed, the noon hay or turn-out, and the evening feed. This is a never-changing framework for me. The rest of my life revolves around it. When in the barn to feed, to prevent a slip-up, I always do everything in the same order. For me, it is dump the grain, put the hay into the two mangers, fill the two water buckets, rake the manure from the two stalls and scoop it into a nearby pile, and tie up Lulu so she doesn't try to steal the greater amount of grain fed to Lucky. After that, I cut up a carrot for each horse, rub a neck or nose (equine), and return to the house.

You may note that Lulu is still tied. I give Lucky an hour to finish his grain and hay and then I return from house to barn

*Removing manure from stalls, a daily job in
any well-run horse stable*

to remove Lulu's halter and take the feed buckets from the mangers. My worry, of course, is that in that hour I will become engrossed in something else and forget to release patient Lulu.

To prevent that, I put the little grain buckets in the middle of the kitchen table, set a minute minder for an hour, and hang another minute minder round my neck, also set for an hour. This sounds like overkill, but it has worked.

Another system other people use relies on establishing the habit, on exiting the barn, of reciting a list of jobs that should have been done, such as: "hay, grain, water, manure, stall doors, lights." Any system, once established, helps to counteract our increasingly unreliable memories.

And then there is the possibility of hiring a stable helper to do whatever tasks have become too burdensome for our bodies. I have been fortunate enough to find younger people in Warwick willing to scoop up the manure pile that I collect from the stalls, as well as that in the pastures during much of the year, and wheel it in a cart or wheelbarrow to where it can be dumped. My husband (eight years my senior) and I did this for years together, until my shoulder operations made scooping up all the manure too risky and pushing the wheelbarrow became too difficult for him. To pay for my stable helper, I take in one or two horses as boarders with the understanding that all I do is feed and water the horse(s) in the morning, at noon, and in the evening, and the owner of the horse cleans up her horse's manure and, depending upon the situation, helps me as necessary with chores I cannot or should not do, such as emptying big bags of grain into large galvanized cans and fixing fences. Everyone's situation is different. I can do the feeding and enjoy this contact with the horses, but I should not or cannot do the heavy tasks, so my current arrangement is perfect. The point is that there are many possibilities out there if we really want to keep our horse(s) at our own barn.

The next option, of course, is to move our horse(s) to a nearby stable where all the barn chores are done for us at a price that may be well worth it, if we can afford the arrangement. For those of us accustomed to caring for our own horses, this can be

31

a very difficult change. As I recount below, I tried moving my horse out for a few months four years ago and just couldn't hack it. Bad withdrawal symptoms. (Again, approximate local costs are given below.)

## Strategies for peace of mind

Ay, there's the rub. We can use all the myriad pieces of equipment available to make us safe and comfortable, and we can employ all possible strategies to compensate for our aging bodies, and yet we wonder if we really *should*, if we really *want* to continue to ride, and possibly if we honest-to-goodness still *can*. Our bodies will recuperate more slowly from a fall. Our reflexes may be slowing. This and that hurts when we ride. Owning horses is expensive, and our income may be less than before retirement. We have less energy each year. All these considerations are valid, but they are usually not central.

The central or most frequent problem, as I see it, is the generally decreasing confidence (noted above) that comes with aging, sometimes disguised but usually discernible. How do we deal with this? We who are over seventy do not need to experience another fall to find that we have less confidence (not to mention daring) than we had in our youth.

So what do we do about it? First of all, we admit our lack of confidence to ourselves if not to our equestrian friends. I have noted that few of the elder riders whom I interviewed actually mentioned diminishing confidence while riding, and yet I sometimes discerned it beneath the surface of what they were telling me. There seems to be sort of a conspiracy on the subject, as if to admit fear will make it more real, and in a sense this is so. "Ignore it, and it will go away," and actually sometimes it does. After which, that small success can lead to more successes, and presto—no fear. Professional trainer and author Gincy Self Bucklin, in an essay on her website, puts it this way: "Confidence—the real deep down stuff that makes for a wonderful ride—is built on itself." The problem is sufficiently widespread for Gincy to run an on-line workshop called the "Riding with Confidence egroup," which consists of riders trying to gain confidence through a day-by-day reporting of their problems and offering each other advice.

It may be, of course, that a rider's lack of confidence is well founded. If you put a rookie rider on a nervous horse, even if that rookie has all the confidence in the world that she can ride well, disaster is likely. The best source of confidence is being able to ride competently, which might require lessons, particularly for someone returning to riding after the hiatus often associated with raising a family.

Another help toward confidence is riding often, without long in-between times. My own nervousness before riding decreases with the frequency of my rides, which is a semi-annual problem because I no longer ride in the summer (too hot and buggy) or in the winter (ice under the snow). The more I ride, the more confident I feel in advance; and conversely, the less I ride, the more likely I am to fret about it ahead of time. I don't know if my experience with ahead-of-time fear, nervousness, lack of confidence—whatever we want to call it—is unusual, but I suspect it is not. For me, the remedy is to ride often, at least twice a week. In between, however, I sometimes ask myself, "Why are you doing this? Why don't you just quit riding?" I haven't been able to answer that question. I hope that writing this book will help me do so.

My personal ahead-of-time problem is not about falling so much as it is about whether I have the energy and desire to prepare for riding and then for the ride itself. My riding buddy for that day will have taken care of the first part, quietly and efficiently tacking up both our horses, thus eliminating both the strain to my uncoooperative shoulders and the extra physical effort. For years I tacked up for the neophyte and returning riders who used to accompany me, and now I am fortunate enough to have it done for me. An experienced and helpful riding buddy is a great asset.

I worry little about hitting the ground, possibly because I have been fortunate enough to mostly stay aboard over the years. My last fall was three years years ago at Lake Dennison, when Lulu as lead horse trotted out into an opening and suddenly, whoops—she did a 180-degree turn. Possibly this occurred as I was on the upbeat of a post, but at any rate I found myself on the ground before I knew it. A hoof had hit me in the middle of my breastbone, and I hurt afterward for a week or so, but I was easily able to remount and ride the hour back to our trailer. I was shaken, but I have ridden long enough to know that if you are going to ride horses, a fall is somewhere in your future.

The next time I rode, it was my turn to ride the more reliable Lucky, which gave me confidence, and for a while when I rode Lulu, I asked my riding buddy to lead on Lucky. By now, I may take the lead even when on Lulu, really without thinking about it. Once mounted, I am good as gold, the queen on her steed, fully in charge, relaxed, and "out to see the world." (Do you remember that phrase from the Mancini song "Moon River"? The next phrase is, "there's such a lot of world to see." And there surely is.)

For riders who have a more pervasive lack of confidence focusing on the actual mounted experience, the pros suggest some sensible remedies. Susan Harris, in an article titled "Rebuild Your Confidence" (*Equus*, October 2009), discusses the topic thoroughly. She points out that the nervousness of a rider transmits itself readily to a horse, thus increasing the likelihood of problems. Among possible remedies she mentions: riding in a controlled area such as an arena, rather than on the trail; breathing deeply when fear begins; going back to the basics of training with your horse; riding only a quiet and reliable horse until confidence returns; and asking for help from a trainer.

An excellent article on fear when riding appears in the September 2008 issue of *Horse Journal*. The author John Strassburger, the performance editor of the magazine, is apparently no longer young, because he has "decades of experience in eventing, steeplechasing, dressage, and fox hunting." He writes of the "comfort zone of a small ring." Amusingly (and perhaps condescendingly) he says that "dressage and the other ring-bound horse sports are the most popular because they welcome riders who fret over guiding their horses anywhere not encircled by a fence." He advises, as with any other anxiety, that "you do it, and you do it again and again until you feel comfortable and then confident." And he suggests that you take one step at a time. I would add that choosing an experienced riding buddy also helps, because not only will you know that, if a problem occurs, you will have knowledgable and efficient help, but a buddy's confidence can sometimes be contagious.

### Practical matters

A few words about relative costs might be helpful, both for riders looking for less challenging alternatives and also for those in their middle years who are thinking about getting back into the sport. Some people once retired have more time to spend on riding, but on the other hand less money. Others, more fortunate, find that their retirement income is sufficient to expand their hobbies and pleasures, and they take the approach that they might as well now enjoy their hard-earned treasure. Still others in their middle years, free of the expenses of educating their children, feel that it is their time to realize their long-delayed desire to ride or drive.

The estimates below are just that—estimates, and quite rough. They represent information gathered primarily in the

Athol-Orange-Greenfield area in Massachusetts during spring 2010. The nearer to Boston and Worcester, the higher the costs. First, for general comparison, I shall report what it costs me personally to keep two horses on my own property in Warwick, which is probably not too far off from what costs are for other riders in my area who, like me, are not indulging themselves and their horses in lots of extras.

With a two-acre pasture and two horses in 2009, my records show that I spent a total of almost $7,000 that year on horse-related items. This total breaks down into the following: hay, $1,300; grain, $1,300; pasture maintenance, $1,000; supplements, $100; stable help, $1,500; blacksmith, $750; veterinarian, $400; miscellaneous, $500. No major equipment or unusual veterinary services were required that year. Riders with large acreage fit for pasture obviously will spend less. Note that the cost per horse is about $300 per month.

The cost of boarding a horse varies widely according to what is offered. An individual stall in a barn plus feeding twice a day might cost as little as $150 a month, but this arrangement would include little else, except perhaps access to nearby trails and an exercise area. The boarder would be responsible for hay, grain, bedding, and clean-up. (This is the board that I myself offer.) In the middle of the cost spectrum, full board at a reputable local stable I contacted is available for $350 a month. At the high end, where everything but everything is offered, the cost might be as much as $450 a month. This price would include not only hay, grain, and regular clean-up but such amenities as regular turn-out, outdoor rings, an indoor lighted arena, hot water, heated tackrooms, and the availability of lessons and training. Such a boarding facility would also provide the sociability of other riders and occasional equestrian events, whereas the less expensive offers privacy and a more hands-on relationship with one's horse.

To my surprise, there is not as much difference per horse per month as I would have thought: about $300 for a simple set-up like I have for my own horses (including, for me, $50 per horse for stable help), and about $450 for the works. The above estimates do not include the considerable expenses that might be required for an injured or sick horse.

For the returning rider or the older rider who has lost confidence, lessons may be just the ticket. I have always felt that group lessons are particularly helpful, in that they provide an opportunity to watch another person being given pointers and also to relax a bit between periods of personal instruction. For lessons, most important perhaps is one's relationship with the instructor, a highly personal matter; and next is the number and age of one's fellow students. Private lessons run about $40 to $50 for an hour and about $30 for a half-hour. Group lessons cost about $30 to $35 for an hour and about $20 for a half hour. Most local stables that I contacted are quite adaptable in the type of lessons they offer. Some but not all stables might offer adult group lessons, which is what I personally would choose. Who wants to compare themselves to the young in nerve and learning speed?

A rider may have lost confidence primarily because her beloved horse, whom she trusted implicitly, has—of all unforeseen things—dumped her. She suddenly may have lost confidence in her horse, which may lead to a general lack of confidence in her own riding skills. The primary question is why the horse behaved as he did. There may be physical reasons, as simple as a misplaced saddle causing irritation on the horse's back to an insect bite or to a not-yet diagnosed physical problem. Perhaps the horse hasn't been ridden for a long time and is feeling his oats, or it may be that he hasn't yet learned that a mailbox won't attack him. Whatever the cause, if he has lost the confidence of his rider, now is the time for a professional diagnosis, first by the vet, of course, but then by a trainer.

The cost of having professional trainers diagnose and hopefully cure a horse of his problem is not as high as one might think, considering both that trainers themselves risk taking a fall and also that they might have to spend considerable time riding and training the horse. I found one quote of $350 a month plus board of $350 a month. I would imagine the owner would then be wise to take several lessons on that horse to restore her confidence in him.

There are dressage lessons for those who not only feel more secure in an enclosed riding area, but also are interested in the subtleties of physical communication between horse and rider. Private dressage lessons are priced at about $55 for 45 minutes, and $45 for 30 minutes at one well-known stable in this area. Interesting, is it not, that dressage lessons are shorter than regular everyday riding lessons, undoubtedly because of the intensity of concentration required by the student—and horse. Semi-private lessons cost $35 per person, again for only 45 minutes.

The choice to drive requires more expenditure for equipment, starting with the cart or carriage, the harness, and a trailer large enough to transport both horse and cart or carriage. A new, lightweight cart and synthetic harness can be bought for about $1,000, but it is quite possible that secondhand equipment could be found for less, particularly if the horses are "minis." Websites offering all types of carts and harness abound. Training costs for beginning drivers are similar to those for riders, beginning at about $40. If the horse is to be trained by a professional, board would be an additional expense, totalling somewhere around $700.

## Discovering What Lasts

The horsemen and horsewomen for whom this book is written, and certainly those interviewed (with perhaps one or two exceptions), do not merely like or enjoy horses. Riding horseback is not just what we happen to do for a sport. We have a *passion* for horses, and this passion makes the retreat from riding and other active ways of enjoying them difficult. Remember Elizabeth Barrett Browning's famous lines: "How do I love thee? Let me count the ways."

Whereas horses for many, many years were used primarily for war, transportation, and work, as they still are in some developing countries, people early on devised myriad ways of playing with them that still survive and thrive. Think of how many sports center on horses. Those that come to mind include, in addition to trail riding: Thoroughbred racing, Standardbred racing either trotting or pacing, polo, jumping competition, cross country, eventing, fox hunting, carriage driving, competitive trail riding, endurance trail riding, equitation shows, dressage, various forms of Western competitions, and no doubt others with which I am unfamiliar. The sports leading that list are appropriate only for those who retain full strength and mobility, in other words, the young.

So let us now count the ways we love, enjoy, and play with our horses, considering one by one the pleasures they provide and also thinking about which we personally may soon have to relinquish, which we might help last a bit longer, and which indeed will stay with us the rest of our lives.

### Riding horses

For those of us fortunate enough to have been physically able to ride and to have led lives in which horseback riding has been a major part, riding trails has usually been a relaxing type of pleasure. Even if our major type of riding is competitive, as in an arena, in a show ring, on a racing track, or on hundred-mile trail rides, at the end of the day most of the competitors among us enjoy an hour or two simply exploring or enjoying familiar woodland trails on our special, well-loved horse. I think this is particularly true for those of us lucky enough to live in the forested portions of Massachusetts.

Part of the pleasure in trail riding derives from feeling one with the horse, a sort of interspecies relationship. We are dominant predator atop submissive prey animal, our legs, hands, and posture sending signals not only of left and right, stop and start, walk and trot but also of confidence and relaxation, a unique camaraderie based on mutual understanding and trust. If the horse is our own, fed and cared for in our own stable, the experience is even more meaningful. For me and many others, this is bliss.

In the disciplines of equitation and dressage, communication between horse and rider achieves a degree of explicitness rarely called for on the trail. Particularly in dressage, every slight movement of the rider requests a response from the horse. Because the commands of an experienced dressage rider are rarely visible to an observer, the language they speak to each other has the intimacy of being shared and secret. I have never attempted dressage, but in observing and speaking with those who enjoy the sport, I can readily imagine its special rewards. For those whose equitation endeavors not only include but specialize in jumping, the cooperation of horse and rider required for safety involves considerable athletic skill and judgment from both. The face and body language of a horseman completing a successful jump speaks clearly of joyous satisfaction with both himself and his horse.

For persons using horses in their everyday work, like those patrolling city streets, cutting and hauling fresh-cut lumber, rounding up cattle, and providing carriage rides, there must also be a relationship as with a buddy. There the emphasis is on cooperation and communication seasoned with the pleasure of everyday companionship.

And then there is the completely different reward that comes with horse and rider experiencing as one the exhilaration of speed. This is less a matter of communication than of sharing an animal pleasure with a member of another species. We both enjoy a good run. Many people, like most horses, revel in speed. For the horse, a run with those of his own species is even more pleasurable, and on his back we ourselves sense the herd instinct. Hence the thrill of riding in a fox hunt. This is heightened by our being aware of how we are cooperating with the horse as we approach and (hopefully) fly over fences and coops. As I mentioned earlier, I thoroughly enjoyed fox hunting in Maryland in earlier years, and a very fast and furious hunt it was. I remember once counting that we had taken twenty-one fences in a morning.

Driving seems to be an up-and-coming sport these days. It ranges from driving a simple cart down a country road with a familiar horse, possibly a Fjord or pony, to driving a pair of specially bred and highly trained Morgans or Trakehners in a carriage-driving competition. Pleasures include viewing the countryside, cooperation, and sometimes speed.

All forms of racing competitions (such as in an arena, cross country, on a track, on a trail, in a stadium) no doubt provide similar rewards in terms of cooperation with the horse and the exercise of mutual athleticism, of course heightened by the hope of glory and monetary rewards in winning. Competition can for some people (not me) sharpen the pleasure of riding, and this certainly applies to certain forms of trail riding. Endurance and competitive trail riding, as well as competitive carriage driving, have many devoted followers where sociability with each other mixes with enjoyment of nature, cooperation with their horses, and testing of their health and stamina. And, primarily in the western United States, rodeos, competitions in rounding up cattle, and similar practical work-based riding form an important equestrian sport that involves all the possible joys of riding.

All these varied and multiple pleasures of riding our horses (relaxation, companionship, cooperation, communication, and the exhilaration of speed and competition) depend upon our health and energy. Fast-moving and competitive equine sports will disappear from our lives first, requiring as they do a rider's physical soundness, strength, and stamina. Trail riding, with a reliable horse, on a comfortable saddle, with an experienced companion, and on familiar trails will probably provide pleasure quite far into our old age. Similarly, dressage with a reliable horse, on a comfortable saddle, with an experienced trainer, and in a familiar arena will probably be enjoyable even longer. And as mentioned above, driving is another option, again with a reliable horse and after obtaining some help from a trainer, because communication is solely through reins and voice. Driving may be the answer when pain makes riding no longer fun. Much depends on which part of our body starts to give out first, as well as which equine pleasure tops the list for us.

## Caring for horses

The health of the horses we ride is partially dependent upon the care we give them—which leads to another very distinct and important source of our love of horses—the pleasure we feel while providing that care.

When I moved from suburban Maryland to a village in Massachusetts, I began for the first time to take care of my own horses. Obviously, the time I spent with my horses increased greatly as did my feelings for them, both positive and negative depending upon the particular horse. As I mentioned above, I now have Lucky, a twenty-three-year-old Quarter Horse gelding

42

and Lulu, a fifteen-year-old Norwegian Fjord mare. Both are easy to work with, both seem to enjoy being stroked, and they have a strong bond to each other. Lucky is the boss, but he needs Lulu near him.

These horses have become my pets in a way that my stabled horses were not. I see them at least three times a day to provide for their care. This constant proximity has made a great difference in my relationship with them. I have come to feel strong affection for both. For Lucky, the affection comes mainly from my trust in him both on the trail and in the barn. His sad eyes, which seem to say, "I have seen it all," the scar on his side probably from overuse of spurs when he was a barrel racer, and the scar on one hind leg prompt me to want to give him special attention to make up for what may have been ill use in his earlier days. For Lulu, my affection is more maternal. Her thick, soft fur almost asks me to pet and hug her, and frequently she will present herself to be petted and hugged. She has the intriguing and sometimes frustrating naughtiness of many ponies, playing with heated water buckets and destroying whatever isn't nailed down (and recently even something that was).

While I have come to love these horses, I do not delude myself into imagining that they love me back. They trust me and are comfortable in my presence, which is their way of returning my affection. Giving love provides even greater pleasure than receiving it. Horses, like dogs, present us with this opportunity. We have an understanding, my horses and I, person to horse and vice versa; when I mount, I change from loving mom to demanding herd leader. This seems to be fine all around, with the dominance question settled to everyone's apparent satisfaction—most of the time.

Caring for horses may also involve breeding, which I have never tried nor wanted to do with any of my mares, although I do understand the nurturing instinct that makes some horse people, particularly women, wish to do this. Tiny foals are, of course, adorable. And then they start to grow up and the issue of training begins. I am interested in all the theories of how to do this that are currently very popular in equine magazines, DVDs, and television shows. I follow the successes (and failures) of some of my friends who have young horses, but I have never had the time—nor really the wish—to bring up or seriously retrain a horse. I have always attempted to purchase reasonably well-trained (but inexpensive) horses, meaning those that understand the basics and have a respectful attitude. In my earlier years in Maryland, when every trail ride included several jumps in and out of fields and woods, I also required horses with some jumping experience so they could handle a three-foot fence without qualms.

So how long can we enjoy caring for our horses? Perhaps as long as our legs oblige us by taking us to and from the barn a few times daily. Or as long as we can pay for someone else to do all or part of the work for us—as I am now doing. For me personally, I think this will be the pleasure I cling to the longest and will eventually give up with the greatest regret.

### Delighting in horses

The most obvious and widespread aspect of a passion for horses is delight in their undeniable physical beauty. Coffee table books with pictures of various breeds, drawn or photographed, are popular with everyone, horse lover or not. Equestrian events draw thousands of people who (in addition to betting) just enjoy watching horses in motion as well as the skill of their riders. Beauty being in the eye of the beholder, many horse lovers find its echo in the commonest of horses, perhaps in the shape of just one physical part and sometimes only in the hint of a more appealing form.

I have often just stood and stared at Lucky, my aging and mixed-breed Quarter Horse, as he munched his grain. I would find myself admiring the muscular development in his back legs or the way his rather scrawny tail catches the sunlight until it seems made of golden strands. As horses go, he is not a beauty, and I knew this very well when I bought him for what seemed (and in fact did turn out to be) a quiet temperament. While not the most beautiful of horses himself, my Lucky echoes the beauty inherent and possible in the breed. I enjoy simply looking at him. The same is true with Lulu, although in a very different way. I am amused watching her march around, seeming to take pride in her ample girth, and I melt simply looking at her big brown eyes.

Not only are horses' shapes, colors, and sheen attractive but also their graceful movement. Again, some more than others. Even people with no particular interest in horses will tune in to the Kentucky Derby on television just for the beauty of the horses' bodies and the athleticism of their movement. They will walk up admiringly to a horse on patrol duty in a city. These same people will drive a bit slower when passing a group of horses in a field, and they are the ones who will pause as they walk by my pasture, offer my horses a carrot or apple brought from home just for the purpose, and reach in to touch and talk to them. If I go to the fence, one (often elderly) person may tell me how she always wanted to ride, but it never happened. She may have harbored over the years an unrequited passion for the species.

We who are aging may always enjoy their beauty. If sight fails us, and even if we lose our short-term memories, our remembrance of pleasures with our horses will remain, visible somewhere deep in our minds and hearts.

# Quitting Time

## Without regrets

In September 2009 I read, again in *Equus*, an article by Mollie Eckelberry titled "No Regrets." Mollie had decided it was time to quit. And she said in her title that she had no regrets. I came upon this article about the same time that I had begun to think about interviewing a group of elder riders for this book.

At the age of seventy-eight, Mollie experienced a serious fall that led to her decision ten days afterward to stop riding. She would continue to care for her twenty-year-old horse but not ride him. Her final two paragraphs tell her story eloquently:

> What a gift these years have been. Now I will be thankful just to have my horses here at home with me to care for, play with, and love. It's funny, in a way, because when I was a little girl this was all I ever really wanted.
>
> My decision is long behind me now, and I haven't looked back. I shudder to think that had my last fall ended differently, I might not have had this time with my horses. But now I'll be able to enjoy them for the rest of my life.

Mollie's peace after her decision is something we all want, but we hope not to require a serious, hospital-stay accident like Mollie's in order to quit. Wouldn't it be fine if we could stop riding just one day before a bad fall *would have* happened?

## Deciding

Perhaps we will never have to make a decision to quit riding and / or caring for our horses. It could be that something unexpected or at least not planned will happen that will make the call for us. Perhaps our horse becomes lame and cannot be ridden for months so that we really after that time lose our desire to mount and ride out. It may be that our familiar woodland trail is going to undergo harvesting of its wood so that we will not have access to it during one of our riding seasons. Our usual riding buddy may move away, become sick, or herself stop riding, and we can't find another immediately, so our riding lapses. Or perhaps something happens in our daily life, such as the death of a spouse, that makes riding and keeping a horse impossible or quite impractical. And of course, a debilitating illness or serious injury to our own back, knees, hips, neck, or shoulders may make riding and / or caring for horses on our own property impossible. If for some reason we cannot ride for a year or so, it is highly unlikely we will choose to start again. Regular riding, once we reach our later years, is crucial to continuing to ride.

Or we may have to face making a decision ourselves based on less catastrophic events, looking carefully at the pros and cons of continuing to ride and care for our horses. We then face a slow process, not a decision suddenly made one gray, rainy, cold afternoon, probably about 5 PM, when we are in a funk.

There are certain questions we should ask ourselves. Primary among them is this: If riding and / or caring for horses is no longer a pleasure, if we no longer really look forward to doing it, why indeed do we force ourselves to continue? I think there are at least three reasons. The first is that we have the apparently inborn passion for horses exhaustingly discussed above. We want to be with them for the special joys they have offered us and hopefully will continue to provide, despite any increasing fears and physical restrictions.

The second reason is that our involvement with horses defines who we are, possibly as much or more than our careers. Women riders in my generation may not have had a career as such, often just a job, and sometimes under "occupation" we must write "housewife," perhaps the most important and yet most unappreciated fulltime job of all. Our dedication to horses tells us and others who we are. When horses leave our lives, just who are we? A housewife, a mother, a widow, a caretaker perhaps. To most of us horsewomen, who tend to be assertive characters, that is not enough. I don't know if the definition as "horseman" is as important to men, because at least in my generation they are more likely to have had a clearly defined occupation.

The third reason is that riding and / or caring for horses is how we spend much of our time. It is our particular, reliable, perhaps everyday pleasure. Take that away, and what have we? Many of us, by the time we finally give up horses, will not be physically capable of taking up another active sport to fill the blank. Quiet, even intellectual occupations, don't quite cut it. Reading books, doing crossword puzzles, knitting, and such are not usually defining occupations no matter how much time we may spend on them and how difficult they may be. Unable to feed, water, pet, and groom our horses, we may somewhat salve our hurting instinct for nurturing by acquiring another dog or cat. New interests are not easy to find for those of us in our seventies and eighties. If we have the financial means, now completely free of horse-related responsibilities, we may decide to travel. And so we join the mostly elderly groups who spend winters in Florida and who book group tours to foreign countries. For me, this would be a sad substitute for a life with horses. Fortunately, I think it does work—or seem to work—for some horse people.

As suggested above, there are half-way solutions, depending upon our physical condition, our mental situation (lack of confidence seeping into our relationship with horses), and our budget. We may decide to ride but not care for our horses or the reverse—to care for our horses but not ride. If it is walking to the stable three times a day, carrying water buckets, distributing flakes of hay to each horse, and the many other tasks involved in caring for our horses that are just too physically difficult, then let us either pay someone to help us or move our horses to a nearby stable. But meanwhile, if being on a horse is not painful, and if we really still enjoy it, let us continue the riding while the pleasure lasts.

On the other hand, if riding is painful to various parts of our bodies and if we question our ability to ride safely and with pleasure but we still enjoy caring for our horses, we can make the decision to keep our horses in our barn and either stop riding or perhaps modify where and with whom we ride. The former is what Mollie of the "No Regrets" article decided to do.

In the worst case scenario, in which both keeping our horses at home is beyond our capability and riding on the trail has become physically or mentally too taxing, there still remain options. Perhaps we can ride or take lessons in an arena at the stable where we have moved our horse, or we might rent or lease one of the stable's reliable horses on a regular basis. Another possibility is riding occasionally with a multiple-horse friend who needs an experienced buddy to come with her.

What I am saying is this: we should not give up too soon. I speak as one who knows, because I myself did this, failing properly to consider my options. After the rotator cuff surgery on my left shoulder in 2004, in compensation I overused my right arm with the result that the right shoulder started to seriously pain me. This shoulder had had rotator cuff surgery before, in 1997. I had been told that another surgery for that shoulder was out of the question, so I knew I should no longer try to clean up the manure in my pastures. I am right-handed, so I could not afford to lose use of my right arm for daily living. I figured that this was the end of the horse road for me. I couldn't groom, saddle, or bridle a horse by myself. I couldn't do the cleanup. I couldn't carry buckets of water.

What to do? First, of course, I cried, and then—also of course—I made a few decisions. I would no longer take care of my two horses. I sold the one who had an attitude when it came to cantering. He would put his head down when I requested a canter, virtually saying to me, "Would you like a buck from me, or shall we just trot?" As for the other one, Lucky, I knew his value as a trusty trail horse so decided to board him at a local stable, just in case. After all, I could still ride. I visited Lucky, and I had a young neighbor ride him in the ring at the stable, but I was unable to find anyone reliable with whom to ride, and the trails behind the stable were poor. Several friends helped by picking Lucky and me up in their trailers and going to various other trails to ride. I appreciated this, I enjoyed the riding, but I missed terribly the daily contact with horses that had become increasingly precious.

To rectify the situation, I decided to board two horses in my pasture, but this didn't work out. For a little while, my Lucky joined those horses, but the couple owning them made it clear that they did not want me to help at all around the barn, nor did they want to ride either by themselves or with me. They just enjoyed the caring part of horse ownership. Meanwhile I found, much to my surprise, that my right shoulder was improving enough for me to rake if not lift manure into a wheelbarrow. Furthermore, I discovered that the young woman who had been riding Lucky at the Orange stable was willing to do occasional cleanup for me. All I needed at that point was a second reliable horse and someone to ride with me regularly.

As it happened, a Petersham friend had been inviting me to ride one of her three Norwegian Fjord mares with her. All three horses went well on the trails in her woods: no bucking, no rearing, no stumbling, ready to canter. And they were small animals, meaning that it would be easier to lift a saddle onto their backs. Perfect for my situation, so I decided to take the plunge and buy a Norwegian Fjord. The little mare (whose registered name is Ursula) was trailered to my home in early May on the same day that the boarded horses left. Lucky immediately fell in love with her, and after observing her antics I decided, since she was quite a lulu, that Lulu would be her everyday name. So here I was, back in business with two horses of my own to ride and care for in what I call my "small barn."

I still, however, required a regular riding buddy and the continued services of someone to do barn chores and assorted work in the pastures. For such services, I knew I needed more regular income. I spread the word about, and soon Jean showed up to board her horse Crunchie with me and to help with tasks my husband and I could no longer do. Because Lucky was not about to put up with another gelding in the pasture with his true love Lulu, Crunchie took up residence on the other side of the property in a large combination stall and paddock in my "big barn." And best of all, Jean enjoyed riding one of my horses with me. I had acquired an experienced, reliable riding companion and helper who was also a paying boarder. Talk about luck!

The moral of the story is that we must not give up too soon, because all sorts of possibilities may be out there. We should carefully consider our situation and the options. There may be more out there than we know and certainly more than I have mentioned. And, importantly, we should let friends know our situation so they can spread the word. A fine solution may be just around the corner, as it was for me.

While it would be foolish to give up riding and / or caring for horses too soon (that is, before we have to), it is equally foolish to continue beyond the time when we honest to goodness want to ride. We may not know why we want to stop, but we do know we want to. That is reason enough. We have ridden and cared for horses because we have wanted to, because it has given us pleasure. Perhaps we will experience the "been there, done that" syndrome that affects other parts of our lives and simply turn to an entirely different activity in our later years. At any rate, when something inside us says no and continues to say no for a while, even if it refuses to give a reason, we should listen.

### After quitting

If (or perhaps when) we decide to give up riding and / or caring for horses, we need not, indeed should not, pull away from our riding friends and the equestrian organizations with which we have been associated. I suspect there will be an immediate sympathy for our new horseless situation, but it will not last long, people being what they are. ("Laugh and the world laughs with you; weep and you weep alone.") This would be the time to become more, not less, active in horse organizations. There are jobs a-plenty in most, some that can be done from home, some that do not require physical exertion, and perhaps some that cry out for our particular talents. All equestrian associations need more people to attend their events, buy their tickets, and provide financial assistance. It is important that we retain our connections to the horse world. After all, we have been and still can be part of it if we make the effort. Having continued with our sport into our seventies, we may be surprised (and somewhat amused) to discover that we are viewed with considerable respect and even admiration by younger riders.

Even after giving up riding, we remain horse people. I think our psyches will suffer less if we acknowledge to ourselves that we retain our passion for horses. Not only should we attend whatever equestrian events we can and provide aid to the organizations, but we should also continue to subscribe to horse magazines, read books about horses, and watch television shows about them. These seemingly bland activities will nevertheless help us retain a sense of our identity as horse lovers.

And do you remember, from my earlier discussion of the various ways in which we love our horses, that the most lasting is delight in their beauty? Despite severe physical limitations, this remains. We should hang pictures of horses on our walls and proudly display pictures of ourselves with our horses so that as we walk through our homes, we can glance at them and think, "Oh my, what beautiful creatures horses are. I do love them still." Even if our sight has not remained the best and we see the pictures a bit fuzzily, nevertheless we know from earlier years how beautiful the horses in those pictures were, how much pleasure they gave us, and how we still love them. We remember.

Memory. There is a new type of memory, often more accurately termed "remembrance," that comes as a special gift to the elderly, not fully appreciated until we ourselves have begun to receive it. Of course we remember the past before we age, but not in the way that comes to us if we live long enough. Kids memorize vocabulary lists and multiplication tables, young people buzz from one remembered task to another, and the middle-aged fuss and worry that they will not remember names and tasks anymore, making and losing lists all over the house and stable. We elders eventually lose our facility to remember lists of things, we forget the next task, and we certainly do not remember names. Those types of memory are for the younger people. We had them, too, at the appropriate time.

Now, however, compensating for the loss of certain types of memory, we are offered a new kind that can pervade and enhance our life. Some people tend to resist this new remembering, this "remembrance," but they shouldn't. The young often misunderstand it, asking us why we tell "the same old stories" over and over again. They do not realize that we are sharing with them precious jewels of our lives. It is also worth noting that when we tell of our past daring exploits on horseback, we are not merely recalling a fact. For a brief moment, we are experiencing it all over again in our mind, visualizing where we were, feeling the movement of our horse under us, and experiencing the excitement and joy of a particular moment, but without the danger of the original. Similarly, when we speak of the fire and beauty of a special horse we owned, we see him in our mind's eye galloping across a golden field, tail high, and then we relive the sensation of moving our hand down over his shining flank.

Think back to Mollie Eckenberry and Miss Em, whose stories were told above. Both experienced the remembrance gift. Mollie wrote in her seventy-eighth year, after deciding to ride no longer: "I have ... compiled a huge mental scrapbook I can leaf through, filled with memories ranging from the sublime to the ridiculous, the tragic to the hilarious." In the article about Miss Emily Ravenal Farrow (Miss Em), the author said that "her memories are as clear as movies in her mind." When asked if she remembered her first horse, Miss Em said:

> It was a pony. I remember the day my daddy brought that pony home in the car, his head sticking out one side and his tail sticking out the other. We didn't have closed cars and the pony was just riding in the back. I can see the car coming down the long drive. [My sister and I] laughed and ran out just to get a look at a pony in a car.

Remembrance is a gift that not only provides us keen pleasure but also may gradually bring with it a depth of understanding of life, a type of wisdom. I just glanced back at the section I wrote on "Remembering and Musing" in *Aging Well: Exploring the Land of Our Later Years*. I was looking for quotations from that book that would also be appropriate here. This earlier book was published in 1999, when I was only sixty-nine years old. I had written it to find out for myself what my own later years might be like and thus to guide myself in preparing for them. I did find some relevant wisdom from poet Malcolm Cowley, written at the age of eighty—the age I happen to be now: "What passes through the minds of many is a stream of persons, images, phrases, and familiar tunes. For some that stream has continued since childhood, but now it is deeper; it is their present and their past combined." I also noted this description of the remembrance faculty of old age by novelist Alice Thomas Ellis in *The Summer House*: "Each new happening is not new, but an echo, a reminder, or a repetition of something that has happened before—and quite possibly before that, and before that again."

Possibly because we who have reached the age of eighty have experienced so much, our minds are becoming full not only of memories but of ideas, which now more than ever connect with each other and lead to new perceptions about life. It is almost as if all those firing neurons, instead of firing according to the established pattern of younger years, now are free to fire differently and to form unusual relationships with each other that lead to new concepts about living. The result is a deepening of how we understand life that may lead to a type of wisdom that can accept more readily what must be accepted—primarily the aging of our body and the restrictions it imposes.

Wisdom does not see in black or white, this but not that, my way or no way. It searches for possibilities for adapting to what life brings. And beyond that, it deepens its appreciation not only for what has been but for what now is. I have been visiting for nineteen years, on a weekly basis, people in their seventies and eighties who can no longer drive a car, who face daily struggles to take even minimum care of their own bodies, and whose lives seem to me very small in scope and variety. I have come to know most of them very well. Some struggle, some whine, some become angry at life. However, there are the few who have the wisdom— the grace—to accept, to adapt, and to appreciate what life has put before them both in the past and in the present. When the time comes for all of us horse lovers to pull back from the many pleasures we have known in riding and caring for our horses, may we have gained enough wisdom to do likewise.

Accept, adapt, and appreciate. Three A's. Do you think that list is short enough for us elder horsefolk to remember it?

# Part II
## Twenty Celebratory Sketches

*The author at 75 astride Lucky, a 23-year-old Quarter Horse she has owned since 2001*

## Presenting the Twenty

What fun and games I have had, visiting twenty of Massachusetts' elder horsemen and horsewomen. I have learned from these horse lovers, first of all, that our passion does not die when our hair turns gray. I also received some very practical advice, some noted in prior pages and other bits and pieces within the sketches themselves.

I put out the call for interviews in the fall of 2009, first to friends in the equestrian organization in which I have been active, the New England Equestrian Center of Athol (NEECA), then gradually to people in other equestrian associations in New England, and one person led to another. The first requirement was that an interviewee be at least seventy years old and have continued to ride or drive into her or his seventies. (There is one exception to this, but she was included because her close involvement with horses continues.) Most were still riding at the time of the interview, and one was only sixty-nine but thinking hard about becoming seventy, as does everyone at that age. None was a professional in the strict sense of the word although a few do or did earn money in the equestrian business.

A second requirement was that the person live in Massachusetts and within two hours' driving time from my home in Warwick, Massachusetts. This requirement was for my convenience, because I thought it important that the interview be conducted in person. (Again, there is one exception, but she lives just across the border and trains in Massachusetts.) I am not keen on driving long distances to unknown territory by myself nor on having an extra person present during an interview. Neither did I want to interview by telephone, because so much more can be learned from visiting at a person's home, possibly seeing the horse(s), and always reading facial expressions and body language. This is particularly true if part of the discussion concerns aging and its often less-than-pleasant consequences. I hoped and discovered that I would not have to travel into Boston or Worcester or into far corners of the state, although all sections of the state are represented. I was somewhat hindered by the departure of many elder horse people into warmer areas during winter months, notably to Florida and the equestrian community in Aiken, South Carolina. Most do not return until mid-April, too late for inclusion in this book.

While all the sketches are of elder riders and drivers living in Massachusetts, the issues facing those in other states, especially in the eastern half of the United States, will be similar.

I tried to interview at least a few people from all disciplines in which elders were likely to be riding. More than half are primarily trail riders (pleasure or competitive), but dressage, equitation, driving, Western, and even fox hunting are also represented. I wanted interviewees from all sections of Massachusetts within my radius, and I succeeded quite well. Only in the far southwestern part of the state was I unable to locate appropriate interviewees. Of the twenty horse people interviewed, six are men and fourteen are women, not a surprising proportion.

I purposely conducted my interviews within a very loose structure. I asked my subjects about their early riding, their occupation, their favorite horses, their present riding or driving, and how they felt about stopping eventually—or in several cases, after having stopped. All structure was soon lost, as a mountain of information, festooned with stories, poured forth about this horse and that (usually in no chronological order). Ofttimes my notes were confusing when I returned home and wrote the first draft, and I had to ask for clarification. I pretty much let my interviewees carry the ball, which they were willing to do. We all have fun talking about our horses and the good and bad times we have had riding and caring for them. I have found in my years of interviewing for various purposes that letting the conversation flow naturally catches more of the flavor of the person than trying to fit him or her into a pattern—and often missing what is special and distinctive about that person.

I was amused, but not surprised, by the responses of most persons interviewed when I sent them my quick first draft of the sketch, with a request that they correct any inaccuracies and add any information or stories that they had forgotten to tell me during our interview. Most sent me considerable new material, including partial rewrites. I think they recognized that what I record here may be the only histories of themselves as riders that their riding friends and acquaintances will read, and they want their adventures to be told "just right." So would I. Herewith I apologize for any inaccuracies that may have crept into the final sketches. Ages are given at the time of my interview with a particular rider, between fall 2009 and spring 2010. I have respected the wishes of my interviewees insofar as I could, inserting where appropriate, cutting where necessary, and rewriting volunteered paragraphs to maintain the conversational style of the sketches. Because that is what these pieces are—simply sketches.

I also requested two pictures, one of the rider with an identified horse and the other showing clearly the rider's face, with the age identified on both pictures. Most of us over seventy are not likely to have recent close-up pictures of ourselves that we want to share. My only request was that the picture have been taken at an age above forty, when character begins to show more clearly on the face. I was pleased with the pictures I received and hope that they will help reveal the very different personalities. Unfortunately, because of design or technical concerns, some pictures I would have liked to use have been excluded.

So here they are, the elder riders and drivers we celebrate, a varied and enthusiastic group, blessed (or perhaps cursed?) with a long-lasting passion for that beautiful and powerful animal, the horse.

*Dan Rice at 71 moving out on his Morgan,*
*Secret Autumn Twilight*

# DAN and CAROL RICE

## Age 76
## Hubbardston

In a deeply forested area of Hubbardston, up a dirt road on a hill, amid stands of tall pine, sits a small brown house. Beyond on one side is what looks like a brown playhouse, and a bit farther on a spacious brown barn appears with two paddocks close by. There is little sun, almost no green. What one sees instead of gardens and plantings are sizable rocks piled artistically here and there, with the focal point being a Stonehenge-like arrangement of rocks in a dirt circle in front of the house. What have we here, thought I?

There were further surprises. Several people had told me that I simply *had* to interview Dr. Dan Rice, who did a lot of horseback riding and had even completed a hundred-mile trail ride a few years ago. I was assured by two young women that he must be in his mid-eighties. This "aged man" greeted me at the door and introduced me to his wife, Carol. Clearly, they were not in their eighties, although possibly only several years away.

Dan seated himself on the floor supported by a couch and cushion, and shortly at my request his wife joined us and arranged herself in the same way. I have long since given up sitting on the floor, so I chose to sit on a chair where I could more easily take notes. The surprise was that although I was there to interview Dan, Carol is clearly just as expert a horse person as Dan. I had been alerted to him and not her because he rides in many scheduled pleasure rides and has therefore been more noticeable. Our conversation soon showed me, however, that she has been a major force in their horse-filled lives.

It was Carol who rode as a child and owned her first horse at thirteen years of age. This was a Morgan, and it is to that breed that both Rices have since given their love, admiration, and time. They now own six horses, four kept at their own stable

65

and two at their trainer's. While both ride their horses, Dan is the one who is seen weekends riding with groups, sometimes from Barre, while Carol is more involved with Morgan shows and driving. They own several carts of different kinds. Their trainer, Tim Morrell, prepares their horses for carriage dressage shows, which they both eagerly attend. Their home is heavily beribboned with the recognition their horses have received at such shows. They also have done some breeding of Morgans.

*Carol Rice at 71 astride her Morgan, Secret Autumn Ashlee*

Dan spent most of his life as a small animal veterinarian and claims it was his wife who inspired him to become a vet after four years in the Navy. He established his own veterinary clinic in Holden in 1969. He sold the business at the age of seventy-three and subsequently worked part-time for the new owners for two years. Dan is a dedicated trail rider, not only on weekends but regularly midweek with friend Alicia, when he may be out for almost two hours. In the winter, when most riders sit by the fire, he will clear part of the trail by tromping it down with snowshoes or by pulling a weighted toboggan behind him. About forty-five acres are usually ridable in the area surrounding the Rices' home, and Rutland State Park is not far away. The highlight of his trail riding life was completing a hundred-mile competitive trail ride in 2003, at the age of seventy. Dan has also judged at ECTRA (Eastern Competitive Trail Riding Association) trail rides.

Physical problems coming with age have perhaps slowed him down a bit but certainly not stopped him. He likes what he calls "competitive" horses, which is the word he uses instead of "hot" or "challenging." (So does she.) He cannot indulge himself too much with such horses because he has congestive heart problems. Perhaps the most annoying feature of his aging has been knee difficulties. He rides with a right knee that has been completely replaced and is somewhat stiff. His left knee should be replaced, but he has decided against that procedure so far, simply because it is that knee that must be sufficiently supple to get him onto his horse. First things first, apparently. And then there is the osteoporosis that gives him a slightly bent-over posture. As he puts it, and wife Carol agrees regarding herself, "it all depends on how badly you want to ride." When asked about the element of fear that he will be seriously hurt if one of his horses somehow dumps him, he admitted that it is riding all the time that banishes fear for him.

Dan has a schedule that keeps him well occupied when not on horseback. He arises at 4 AM, arrives at his gym when it opens at 5 AM, does his exercise there, and then takes a walk along the streets of Holden. After that, he may head in to participate as a volunteer at the New England Assistant

Dogs Services, where he not only does such veterinarian tasks as giving shots but also participates in the more lowly requirements of such a facility. He does this two days a week.

By the time I had learned all this about Dan, I was beginning to realize that Carol had been just as thoroughly involved in the buying, breeding, raising, and showing of Morgan horses as her husband. With some prodding, she began to reveal more about her own background with horses beyond the fact that she first owned a Morgan at age thirteen. A picture on the wall shows her grandmother in an informal riding costume. Her mother was also an enthusiastic horsewoman. It was Carol who bid on some of the horses that she and Dan have bought and who made decisions concerning the carts they pull. She also has enjoyed riding throughout her life, speaking lovingly of various horses she has owned and ridden, primarily on the land surrounding their property rather than with groups. She feels safe riding alone, sometimes in the past with her black Doberman accompanying her. She still feels the results of a serious riding accident about ten years ago, so that the first miles of a ride can be painful.

It is primarily Carol who has maintained extensive trails in the area. She seems to enjoy walking out there, often with her horse held loosely by the reins. She clips and saws while the horse grazes on what is within reach. After the December 2008 ice storm, there is considerable clearing to be done, she says. It is also she who has done the rock work that I noted when I first approached the house. Sometimes she will bring home from a trip a rock that she especially likes.

Dan left after an hour or so to move a horse from one place to another and then run an errand. I still felt that I was missing something major about this couple, so I asked Carol if she would show me their horses. This she happily did. I was very impressed by their dark beauty and very Morgan faces. There are four horses to be led into the barn at night, and these are not quiet, completely cooperative beasts. Carol moved one of them inside while I was still there, chain over nose, and even the sliding stall doors took considerable strength to move. She remarked that one of the horses is difficult to lead, so that her

*Carol at 63 with her pack of Siberian Huskies*

husband usually moves him, but that when she has to, she first puts bits of hay along the path from paddock to barn so that he will pause along the way if he starts to get out of hand. Carol is not a big woman but obviously stronger than she looks, fearless, and practical. She and Dan do all the work entailed by the four horses on their property—regardless of the weather. Not bad for people in their mid-seventies!

When we went into the barn, I noted an arrangement on one side that piqued my curiosity. And here came another surprise. Until fairly recently, Carol with her husband had bred and trained Siberian huskies, up to twenty-nine of them for a period of twenty-two years. This was my last surprise of the day, but as I left I was wondering if I had missed something else about this remarkable couple.

*Alyse Aubin at 71, driving My Sweet Prince at the Tub Parade at Orleton Farm in 2008*

# ALYSE AUBIN

## Age 72
## Sutton

Forthright, adventurous, self-reliant, social. Alyse Aubin seems to be having a wonderful time at seventy-two. She is riding horseback with a group of friends three times a week. Once a week she trailers her cart and horse solo to meet an equally stalwart friend and drive at a trot through various state parks. And in between she is cooking for and entertaining friends. Not bad.

Like most of the people I have interviewed, particularly the women, Alyse was onto horses very young. Brought up in Philadelphia suburbs, she was sufficiently horse crazy to—and she swears this is true—walk into the horse manure left by the ragman's horse, just to have the smell of horses near her. That is a pretty bad case of early horse passion. She still keeps the little toy horse, Flicka, given her when she was eight.

Alyse was fortunate in having parents who tried to make horses available to their young daughter and were not fearful about her riding alone in her teen years. Before that time, they took her to Fairmount Stables, where she was introduced to the walk, trot, and canter on a lead line by the groom. When she was ten, the family moved to downtown Worcester, and she was able to rent a horse at the Brown Stables in Cherry Valley. She was allowed to take a horse out by herself and would sometimes just take him for a walk, tie him to a tree, and do "pretend" things. Next there was Pat Rooney's stable in Auburn, and for several summers she went to a girls' horse camp in Roxbury, Vermont, called Teelawooket. When she was fourteen years old, the family moved to Sutton, where they bought a farm so Alyse could have a horse. She is now, almost sixty years later and after being elsewhere for many years, living in that same house and on that same farm—and of course she still has horses.

Alyse's trusty horse of her teen years was Ginger, a twenty-two-year-old gelding, but ridden by her as if he were much younger. She was always on him, sometimes riding a mile just to join a friend who also had a horse and sometimes riding him to school and tying him to a tree. He had heaves (a respiratory disease), and Alyse remembers now that she and her family didn't know much about horses or what to do with that situation, but somehow Ginger, in spite of being ridden a lot, survived to the age of thirty-five.

Amiable Ginger was also rigged up to be driven. Alyse discovered in a neighbor's barn an old harness, cracked, moldy, and riveted in places. She later found a wagon for five dollars, one of the so-called "Democrats" from Sears and Roebuck. She took the front axle off, put a pillow around it, and hooked the horse to the shafts. She sat on the shaft. And would you believe that Ginger accepted this? Later, he and Alyse went around the neighborhood, with the horse hitched to the wheelbarrow with the moldy harness, while she sold home-baked bread from the old Democrat. Pretty incredible. What a sight to have seen.

Alyse drove Ginger in a more aristocratic manner in the 250th anniversary parade in Sutton. She started at home, drove the four miles to Sutton Center, did the parade route, and then drove him home again. He must have been quite a horse.

Then came college, marriage, and kids, which is the usual time for horses to disappear from a woman's life—if not from her heart. Again Alyse was fortunate in that she was able to ride in Fairmount Park while she was at Moore College of Art in Philadelphia, Pennsylvania. After marriage, she taught art in elementary schools in Lisbon, Connecticut, and then came a gap of about six years without horses. At times since then she was a quality control person at Frito Lay and for eight years worked with monkeys as an animal care technician at the New England Primate Research facility. Stories to be told about that, no doubt, but horses are our subject here.

During her mothering years, Alyse bought Chocolate Chips, a "good old boy" that she still has today. She broke him to harness and drove him many years, even after he became blind. He lived to be twenty-eight years old and is buried on the property. Next came Vanilla Fudge, a six-year-old paint gelding that supposedly could drive but, as it turned out, needed a bit more training. He was okay until she took him into a tree farm where they had to drive over wood chips. He became startled, bolted, threw Alyse and her dog out of the wagon, and overturned it, breaking the shafts. After that experience, he would not allow himself to be hitched ever again. Alyse's teenage son found this an occasion for humor, setting the old broken wagon up on the front lawn bearing a large sign reading "Speed kills." Next came Pickles, a pony mare, that Alyse drove for many years. She says, "Ponies are great fun. They can go anywhere, like ATVs." Pickles was eventually given to an old man to drive with care, because she had a bad case of heaves.

My Sweet Prince, a 12.2-hand pony, was acquired to pay a boarding bill. Alyse "broke him to drive" as well as to ride, and she declares him a joy both ways. He is the pony that Alyse now both rides and drives. She competes annually in sleigh rallies, with My Sweet Prince winning the championship at the rally at Orleton Farms in 2010. In 2005, for the three hundredth anniversary parade in Sutton, Alyse drove Prince in the same parade and on the same route that she had driven Ginger fifty years previously. I do wonder how many drivers can make the same claim—of having driven in the same celebration, in the same town, fifty years apart.

Alyse also drives in the Tub parade in Lenox with a pony cart, and she has won prizes in Fun Day, costume class. She loves the costumes, with her art background contributing to the hats that she makes and the fresh-flower decorations she devises for the horse and cart "Tub" parade. She showed me a few of the gorgeous flowered hats she has worn. Alyse is also a member of the Colonial Carriage and Driving Society and participates in some of its events and competitions.

Alyse has enjoyed group rides, as apart from drives, such as the Cross State Trail Ride, a ten-day ride of about a hundred

*Alyse at 71 driving My Sweet Prince at the Tub Parade in the Fun Day Costume Class at Orleton Farm in 2008*

riders, in which she has participated six or seven times. And, as mentioned above, she rides three times a week for several hours with a local group that calls itself the "Leatherbutts." They ride in various parks within an hour's drive, such as Douglas, Arcadia, and Nachaug West Hill Dam. Interestingly and especially to the point here, the group is composed of men and women sixty-two, sixty-four, seventy-two, seventy-six, and eighty-one years old.

Now in her pasture are the tried and trusted My Sweet Prince and also Bow Tie and Tail, a Kentucky Mountain Horse, small, twenty-four years old and bought at ten. She rides the two horses alternately in her three days of riding per week. She drives less often, but it is with the driving that My Sweet Prince excels. A third horse, Homer, has been on the farm for twenty-one years, and Alyse laughingly says that her love / hate relationship continues with him for the sake of her "significant other," who rides him.

I asked Alyse about the wisdom of a rider deciding to take up driving when she finds herself no longer comfortable astride a horse. She said she has known of quite a few people in their fifties and above who have done this successfully, depending of course on the nature of their disability. And she offered some advice. She suggested buying equipment you can handle completely by yourself, such as the Easy Entry metal cart she has owned since the 1970s. By herself, Alyse is able to turn this on its side and lift it into one stall of her two-stall trailer, thus obviating the need for a helper on hand. I tried myself to lift it and was surprised to agree that it really is not impossibly heavy. She also advises using a small horse or pony with a cart that can slip through narrow parts of trails and is easy to hitch up.

Alyse is not pondering about how much longer she herself will be able to ride. Instead, she is trying to think of ways to help some of her elder friends to continue riding. For example, one has a horse with a problem that may make him impossible to ride. She urges finding a friend with two horses and riding one of them. People with two horses (like me) are delighted to find someone competent to ride the second horse. The problem is that as we get older our confidence decreases and we want to ride the same horse all the time, the horse that we have known for years and that we trust (rightly or not). It takes a bit of guts to get on another person's horse, even one that we have observed to be quiet. And the amount of guts we have, certainly in our eighties, is a heck of a lot less than we had in our forties. (I speak from personal experience on this one.) Acquiring a new horse and training it to our particular needs is usually out of the question.

So Alyse is going strong with her horse life. She obviously sees many more years ahead of her for riding, driving, entertaining, and whatever else exciting may come along. You never know what may be around the corner.

*Donald Grypko at 74 on Danny Boy, a Missouri Fox Trotter*

# DONALD GRYPKO

## Age 74
## Greenfield

From the moment I met Donald, I knew I would have an enjoyable conversation. He is clearly upbeat as well as friendly—and loves to talk about the special pleasures of his life, including, of course, horses. The three horses presently on his property were standing in a row to say hello from the fenced wooded area close to his house. They were, however, upstaged by Tucker, his black retriever, whose resemblance to a small black bear is remarkable and who has a penchant for standing on the feet of those from whom he wants attention.

Donald is a seventy-four-year-old farm boy, the seventh of nine children on a farm in South Deerfield. Horses have been in his life for as long as he can remember. His first experience, a vague but not disappearing memory, was of being left as a very young 'un on a horse-pulled flat wagon while his family worked in the cucumber field around it. And yes, you guessed it, the horse for some reason was suddenly frightened and took off at great speed. Of course he headed for the stable and all was well with little Donald—who was, however, sufficiently impressed to remember it for seventy years or so. A similar incident happened when he was twelve or thirteen years old, but this time he was driving the horse when some ground bees surprised it, leaving Donald surprised and on the ground.

Another childhood memory, less traumatic, is of hours spent following a horse pulling a cultivator. The horse knew the job better than his young co-worker, as they together went up one row, turned, and went down the next row. All Donald had to do was lift one part of the cultivator at the end of a row so that the horse could turn it down the next row. The horse even told him when it was lunchtime by simply stopping at the end of a row and waiting to be unhitched and ridden back to the barn.

81

Unlike some farm boys accustomed to horses but not inspired by them, Donald took up Western-style riding as a young man, and he remembers in the years after service as a Marine taking many long rides in the countryside and forests of the area, sometimes alone and other times accompanied by a few pals. He was employed by Western Massachusetts Electric Company, for which he later became a supervisor, but in the early years his job took him throughout central Massachusetts, where he discovered all the back roads and trails that he later would ride for pleasure.

At one point he owned a pure black gelding named Nighthawk, who was sufficiently obedient that generally he could be left standing while his master checked on the safety of the area ahead. Donald tells the story of dismounting to check out a wooden bridge for safety, and while still traipsing carefully on the boards, hearing his buddies yell to him to keep on going and not turn around, because Nighthawk was carefully following him on the bridge and might cease to do so if his master turned. Still another time, he was checking out a tall stone wall to find an opening, only to turn around and see Nighthawk with all four feet on a big flat stone on top of the wall just behind him. This same horse was nicknamed the moose for his ability to find grass to eat even when it was under water or snow. Donald's next two horses were a Palomino and a Buckskin named Dusty, who if not ridden at least every other week would get out of the pasture on his own. Next came a Standardbred named Blackie that Donald used to pull carriages as well as to ride.

Then, at the age of twenty-seven, Donald married Mary, and a whole new life began. He sold Dusty and Blackie. He and Mary had four children, all of whom learned to ride at the nearby stable owned by Valerie Dean. Several horses came and went over the years, the first particularly remembered because his name reflected his odd coloring—Bacon Flour.

Donald continued to ride, but not as much as in his bachelor years. He spent a lot of time at Valerie's, taking his children and sometimes horses over there for shows and doing some show announcing for her. They remain good friends.

In 1978, at the age of forty-two, he purchased Sirach. Donald and his family rode Sirach until he had to be put down at the age of thirty-five in 1995. Donald called him his push-button horse, because he was well-trained and enjoyed performing well at horse shows. He would tease his daughters that Sirach won the blue ribbons by himself, for the horse would listen to the voice commands of the announcer. Is it surprising that part of Donald's e-mail address is "sirach"?

Life abruptly changed for Donald in February of 2004, when Mary's successful hip surgery sparked side events in her body that resulted in severe strokes. For four years, Donald nursed Mary at home until her death in 2007. Donald was not riding during this time. A very spiritually sensitive man, he says that he was sustained through those years by his close relationship with God. He also has faced several major physical setbacks of his own, but his spirit has obviously not been broken.

In fact, Donald has a new enthusiasm—motorcycles. After fooling around with the bikes owned by his children and their mates, he finally got his permit on his seventy-third birthday and now rides the back roads on a Honda Goldwing. This meant nothing to me and perhaps not to a reader, so I will tell you that this bike weighs eight hundred pounds. Sort of horse size, isn't it? Long distance, too. In fact, when I spoke to him, he was planning a weekend bike trip to Prince Edward Island alongside the bike-riding males of the next generation, with the females driving along in cars to keep them company and join in the fun. He obviously enjoys a warm family life.

So, as Donald showed me his big bike with pride, I wondered if he has forgotten horses after all. He remarked that he has never even "looked at giving up" horseback riding. He admits to riding without a helmet, saying, "I suppose I should ride with a helmet but enjoy riding natural." He is currently actively searching for a buckskin Quarter Horse with all the virtues of Sirach. As I was getting into my car to leave, Donald stopped me by asking if I wanted to see his new Australian saddle. Of course I said yes, and he brought out a big saddle and put it on a sawhorse to be admired. In fact, he helped me get onto it there so I could see how wonderfully comfortable it is. Now all he needs is that buckskin Quarter Horse that he just knows is out there waiting to be found.

*Judy Voll with Blythewood Patty in 2009, courtesy of Gary Knoll Photography, as published in* The Aiken Horse, *April/May 2009*

# JUDY VOLL

## Age 75+
## Dalton

Here we have the consummate competitive trail rider, dedicated over the years to piling up the miles, especially in the hundred-mile rides available seasonally up and down the East Coast. Judy has been riding the long ones since 1964 at the Green Mountain Horse Association's (GMHA) hundred miler in South Woodstock, Vermont. In 2000, she completed her hundreth hundred miler.

Judy's approach to these long-distance rides stems from her interest in and her knowledge about anatomy, both human and equine. She graduated with an Associate in Science degree from Becker Junior College in Worcester and immediately landed a job as a laboratory technician with a Pittsfield surgeon. She remained with him until the birth of the first of her four children. This surgeon was a specialist in leg injuries, which perhaps accounts for her present interest and expertise in equine legs. Later she worked for two-and-a-half years for a veterinarian to learn the mechanics of horse movement.

All her children learned how to ride and also to drive, and although none followed their mother down the equestrian trail, all have excelled in some sport, having a strong athletic inheritance from both sides. Their father throughout his life has distinguished himself in various sports from motor boat racing to skiing, semi-pro hockey, and open-water canoeing.

Returning after early-motherhood absence to the work force, for twenty-five years Judy held the position of night medical records librarian at what is now the Berkshire Medical Center, alternating child care and such with her day-employed husband. (On weekends she was on horseback.) About the time of her retirement, she started emergency medical technician (EMT) training, starting with the basic course. She served at the Dalton Fire Department and Ambulance Service for eight-and-a-half years. Wanting to rise in the ranks and assume more responsibilities as an advanced EMT (Intermediate), she trained at Springfield College and moved to the county ambulance service in Pittsfield. She took sufficient training to become a CPR and defibrillator instructor and then an EMT examiner for the Commonwealth of Massachusetts. Judy is also a volunteer at the Windsor Fire and Rescue. (Incidentally, somewhere along the line she met my nephew David Owen, who is an EMT paramedic. He pointed Judy out to me as an enthusiastic and experienced elder rider whom I simply had to interview for this book.)

Judy began her long equestrian career at the age of five with a pony named Jerry. She lived on a farm in Washington, Massachusetts, and she says that she was the horse person on the farm, whereas her brother was the cow person. She rode bareback until junior high school years when she finally saved seventy dollars from a waitress job to buy a cavalry saddle. She attended horse shows as a teenager, but that kind of riding did not particularly appeal to her. She had no interest in going, as she put it, "round and round."

At one of the horse shows, she met two men who were competitive trail riders, and they set her on her long course of trail riding. Judy identified them as the late Len Bull from Lenox and Steve O'Connell from Pittsfield, both hundred-mile riders with GMHA. When she was given a Standardbred named Susie Q in the mid sixties, she was off and running with competitive trail riding, doing her first hundred miler in 1964. Since then she has ridden fifteen times in the Florida 100; thirty-four consecutive years in the Hot Springs, Virginia, 100, placing in all of them; twenty-one times with the New Jersey Trail Riders Association 100; twenty-five times with the New York 100 at Brookfield Fairgrounds; and either ridden, judged, or managed every year from 1964 to 2008 with the

Vermont 100 at South Woodstock; ten times at the Maine 100 in the Norway area; and six times in the New Hampshire 100 at Warner. Including other hundred milers in Maryland, Massachusetts, North Carolina, and Ohio, she holds 112 completion ribbons for hundred-mile competitive rides and two endurance rides. Compute that and you have 11,200 miles. Competitive trail riding has been the heart of Judy's life.

*Judy on Blythewood Patty in Asheville, North Carolina, in 2005, with The Biltmore House on the hill behind*

Judy is one of the Aiken, South Carolina, riders. She owns a small farm there where she spends the winter doing much of her training. She enjoys riding with year-round residents as well as the flock of New England riders who also migrate there for the splendid trails and sociability with other horse people.

In the Ocala, Florida, area in 2001 Judy acquired Blythewood Patty. Out riding, she and a friend met up with Mike, a local resident who mentioned that he was selling all his horses and other stock, including a black Arabian mare who was just too much trouble to care for. She would not come in with the others to be fed, spending her time with an old goat and a donkey, and it was too much trouble to go out and bring her in. As a result, she was starving, so Mike was about to sell her for $500 as horsemeat. Judy told him to wait, and she quickly gathered a trainer and a veterinarian to come out with her that day to look at the horse. She was 14.2 hands, about ten years old, had infected teeth, was just skin and bones, and her hooves were bad, but her eyesight was okay and she seemed sound. The trainer mounted her and found no insoluble problems. Judy bought her there and then, trailered her back to Aiken, and found she weighed in at only 399 pounds—which rose overnight another thirty-five pounds after she drank quantities of water and ate enough hay to satisfy her. After a year's training, the little Arabian was ready for competition. This mare, Blythewood Patty, has been Judy's competition mare ever since.

Over the forty-six years that Judy has been doing competitive trail riding, much of it at hundred milers, she has developed considerable knowledge concerning choosing and training horses for long-distance competition. She has owned and leased quite a few horses over that period. Her first (and not unusual) choice is Arabians, which she has ridden almost exclusively since the middle seventies. She says "their motors are always running," and "they present themselves beautifully." Arabians are well-known for their endurance. Judy says she buys for breeding and attitude and that she trusts the opinion of the vet examining a horse before buying.

Judy has found that each of her horses has been capable of competing in about ten of the hundred-mile competitive trail rides. Having trained numerous horses for long-distance riding, she has definite theories about what works best. Prime among them is that one must begin the training with a hundred miles of walking—no trotting, no cantering. At no more than four miles an hour, that means at least twenty-five hours spent walking the horse before you can let him even trot. Few riders would look forward to that, but Judy herself follows that rule and has found it effective in building the muscle and endurance required for long-distance competition.

Judy has done a lot of lay judging and examining of horses at stops during competitive trail rides. She describes herself as very particular in the matter of cleanliness of both horse and equipment, explaining the harm that can occur to a horse's back from dirt in a blanket or saddlepad. As she spoke about the five things to look for in a horse's leg at the stops, I realized that her knowledge of the horse anatomy is more than superficial.

Not only has Judy ridden on hunded milers, but she has also managed the GMHA's fortieth-year through seventieth-year rides offered at five-year intervals, as well as managing, riding, or judging twenty-one other years. For the past six winters in Aiken, South Carolina, during the eventing season, she has been Chief Jump Judge at Class A events, put together the cocktail and dinner parties, and done other similar responsible tasks. Judy's newest venture is taking driving lessons from one of Aiken's successful driving instructors. Her general upbeat attitude toward riding and the groups with whom she rides is rather well expressed in a little verse she wrote for one of the GMHA events:

> May the sun shine always at your back,
> May the rain forget to fall,
> May you and your horse
> Stay right on the course
> 'Til you're safe and sound
> Back in your stall.

Of course, I asked about the future for Judy. At "seventy-five-plus"—she could not be coaxed or teased into revealing her exact age—how did she see the coming years with horses? This led to a discussion of fairly recent accidents she had while riding. In 2005, she had a very serious spill when several deer ran out in front of her horse. She landed on her arm, broke her ribs, pushing them into her lungs, fractured three vertebrae, and to complete it all, the horse stepped on her face. She was in a cast for six months. This was the year when Judy decided that she would not ride in any more hundred milers. They just were too tiring for her already compromised body. She says she has no pain when riding, but on dismounting, her body really sends her messages. As for potential accidents, she says, "I no longer bounce. I splatter."

And then there was last year's encounter with a bear. Possibly because a nearby trail had to be revised after the December 2008 icestorm and bears were not accustomed to human traffic in the new route, a bear lumbered onto the trail right in front of her horse, who spooked badly. Judy fell into the sharp remains of a downed tree, gouging a chunk out of her right leg and further injuring two vertebrae. There went three months to recuperation. Judy still is limping a bit from that episode—but this hasn't stopped her now from getting up at five in the morning and exercising her horse every day. After all, there was the Virginia fifty miler in May to prepare for.

Judy says she has slowed down with her riding but is not giving it up. She admits that she becomes more tired than she used to, but that she continues to enjoy the "shorter" competitive rides—twenty-five, forty, fifty, or sixty miles—all of which tire me just to think of them. She says she is more choosy about when and where she rides. Judy says, "riding is what I do," and "something drastic" would have to occur to end her riding. Apparently the deer and the bear encounters didn't qualify for her as sufficiently "drastic."

*Whitey Streeter at 44 hunting deer on Patches in 1965*

# LEONARD "WHITEY" STREETER
## Age 89
## Bernardston

Here we have the ultimate old-time horse wrangler sort of guy, at a very lively eighty-nine years of age, with a glint in his eye and stories to tell. Whitey is a Streeter, which in Bernardston is an important name going "away back." He seems to know everyone, and everyone knows him. His father built the Streeter General Store on Route 10 beside a road leading straight (so to speak) down into Greenfield. His uncle, Herman Streeter, who died recently at the age of ninety-eight, was a well-known horseman, as is his nephew Danny.

Whitey was eager to meet me not at his home, as I had suggested, but down at the Bernardston Police Station. He works there in his own office as the town's animal control officer and animal inspection officer. The afternoon I met him there, he had had calls to get rid of a possum and a skunk. After the usual response of "carefully," when I asked how he captured the skunk, he answered "by the tail." Recently, he had been called on by a woman from Greenfield, outside the area of his responsibility, simply because she knew about his expertise and had an Australian Shepherd runaway on her property. Whitey knew where the dog belonged immediately, remarking that if you have been a dog officer as long as he has, you pretty well know where all the dogs belong.

Whitey was one of nine children born to Harold Streeter and the only one who had an abiding and practical interest in horses. His father in 1925 built not only the general store everyone in the area knows as Streeter's, but others throughout New England. His father and uncle also owned and ran a pony farm, selling the animals in that day for forty dollars apiece. Whitey guessed that they must have owned 150 horses—a big operation. He acquired his first pony when he was eight years old, and already he knew how to outsmart man and beast. The pony was mean, but young Whitey wanted him, so he persuaded his brothers to donate to his effort the thirty-five white Peking ducks they owned to use as trade for the desired pony. Early on, he started racing, first at pony races at the Northampton fairgrounds. And, of course, he used horses on the farm. There is a charming picture, unfortunately not sufficiently clear to reproduce here, of him as a very young boy following a horse with a cultivator.

Whitey said that by the age of sixteen he did a lot of wild cattle catching, and an article in a local newspaper in January 1946 called him a "farmer and wild cattle expert." I blinked at that and said something like, "Oh, you went out West?" He grinned and said, "No, no, right here." This was a revelation to me, since in 1946, at the end of World War II, I was living in a mid-sized Pennsylvania town with many dairy farms but surely no wild cattle. Whitey patiently explained to me that ofttimes farmers grazed their cattle in large areas, and when they came to bring them in, there might be one or two missing. He and others were hired to retrieve them. He would take out his carefully trained English Shepherd dog, who would track the missing cattle, with Whitey following on horseback. When the cattle were found, he would do whatever was necessary to get a rope on them, sometimes tying one to a tree while heading back with another. Uncle Herman had the first really good cow dog, named Polly. He bred these English Shepherds as cow dogs and responded to calls throughout New England.

Other wild cattle catchers would go out with Pit Bulls, but their tendency to attack rather than just track a cow sometimes led to harming the cow. At such times Whitey and his dog would be called in to do what was necessary, sometimes taking them when requested to the Streeter slaughter house operated by Whitey and his uncle. And thereon hangs another story about catching pigs to take to slaughter, with the maxim

Whitey repeated throughout our conversation, that you just "gotta be smarter than the pig."

And Whitey was indeed smarter than the pig and, more importantly, than the horses he trained. Racing trotters at pari-mutuel racetracks and training horses were central to his adult life. Trotting races were a very big thing in those days in the areas near Bernardston. There were many farmers with horses eager to see who had the best horse, and there was money to be made if you played it right. He started as a young man and didn't quit racing until the age of seventy, which was the legal cutoff point for drivers at pari-mutuel racetracks.

The hero of Whitey's driving life was a Standardbred colt, Wee Bit o' Scotch, so named because at his birth this was the libation offered. Whitey raced this colt with great success, and when bred, he passed his abilities on to his young. Because he seemed always to be the winner, his races had to be very carefully chosen. Whitey explained the theories of how to make money racing at the track and admitted with a grin to perhaps cutting a few corners during his career. One registered Standardbred mare, named appropriately Trotter, was so fast at both trotting and running that in a certain unofficial event, if the trotting race was in the morning and the running one in the afternoon, he entered the horse in both events and won them both.

Another corner or two was cut as Whitey trained and sold horses. He said that truckloads of mustangs were brought in from the West for selling here, and some of these horses were mean, a word he used often in speaking of horses. He would buy and train these horses for sale to whoever wanted them, and this was a rough and dangerous business. To put it mildly, Whitey was not one to "whisper" to his horses. He did what he felt was necessary to get a horse to understand that he, Whitey, was boss—whatever that would take. Often a bucker would put him on the ground, but that was part of the business, and he says he usually landed on his feet.

And then there was a bucking horse named Chet, a chestnut gelding with a white face. Whitey tried him out in a large enclosure where the property owner warned him not to trample the garden in one corner. When he mounted, the horse started bucking everywhere, particularly in that garden. The owner was so impressed by Whitey's performance that he pardoned the destruction to his garden. And then Whitey bought the horse for fifty dollars. It was that horse that he was able to train sufficiently to sell him for $125, and when he misbehaved for the new owner, Whitey bought him back for fifty dollars. This happened a few times, so he made a buck or two on that one.

Whitey admits to being a bit of a showoff at times. Way back in 1941, when he would have been only twenty-one, he rode a horse (appropriately also named Whitey) down Main Street at a canter, using neither saddle, nor bridle, nor rope. He then parked his horse at a store, went inside for a purchase, and came out to find people gawking at this untied horse and worrying about where it came from and who owned it. With a young man's bravado, he says he just quietly mounted the horse and proceeded home at a slow canter. That same bravado was recorded in the 1946 newspaper article mentioned earlier, which shows him "plunging down a rocky slope" on his horse Patches, with a doe slung behind him in the saddle and his rifle held high in his left hand.

I asked Whitey if he is still riding. Mainly, he says, he now does such things as try out horses and advise people looking to buy one. He often goes down to the auctions at Crowley's in Agawam, as he is a good friend of the owner. In fact, he told me that he was just down there last year with his nephew Danny, when Crowley brought out two horses and suggested that Whitey and Danny enter the flag race. This they did and won. Standing now at somewhat under his former six-foot height, Whitey claims he can still mount from the ground.

I risked asking Whitey the question that I ask all interviewees, even though it seemed silly in this case: "Are you ever afraid?" The answer was, "Hell no!" I proceeded with the question as to whether he ever wears a helmet, and he remarked "I don't know what they are," followed by an admission that he has had to wear helmets as required—which has been on the track, of course. His health is pretty good at the moment although he has had bouts of hernia surgery. He said that at the age of seventy he began to be more careful, out of respect for his aging bones, in deciding what horses he rode. He is not sure he can always land on his feet anymore—in fact he said that one time doing that he broke a foot. Does he ride trails still? Well, not this autumn but the year before, and he would still enjoy doing it even when a group goes out longer than perhaps is comfortable for him.

After all my questions about his current ability to ride, Whitey glanced up at me with a smile and said, "If you want, we can go on down to Danny's place right now, and I can take you out for a ride." Tempting, but I didn't take him up on it.

*Whitey at 89 in his Bernardston animal control office*

*Sue Hellen at 80 sleigh driving with Askepott, her Norwegian Fjord*

# SUE HELLEN
## Age 85
## Petersham

My interview with Sue Hellen was one in which I was particularly interested, because there are provocative similarities in our situations. I knew that she was just a few years older than I, was also a frequent trail rider, and like me had two horses, one of which was also a Norwegian Fjord. Her second horse was an Icelandic, whereas mine is a grade Quarter Horse.

We had met each other casually at events sponsored by the equestrian organization in my general area, NEECA (New England Equestrian Center of Athol). I had sort of been keeping an eye on Sue, wondering at what age she would stop riding, with the vague thought that if she kept on until a certain age, then I might be able to do so also. So when I heard that she was attempting to find suitable homes for her horses, I wanted to know why, wondering if her situation would help me know when to quit. Would I be foolish to continue riding into my eighties? Might Sue's experiences provide any guidance to me? Like many an answer to such a question, the answer is annoyingly vague: "perhaps, just a little."

Unlike me, Sue started riding as a child. Brought up on a farm, she was accustomed to work horses and in fact helped with the farm work. She was allowed to drive the horse used to rake the scatterings of hay left after a first raking, and early on had a riding pony named Sanko. Then came college, marriage, and four daughters, with little opportunity for riding, although she made sure that her children learned to ride. After her youngest daughter entered school, Sue became a full-time elementary school teacher. During this period, the whole family was into skiing and sailing.

It wasn't until the children were all off at college that she and her husband Fred decided to acquire a driving horse so they could enjoy Petersham's back roads together. Her husband was not a rider, but his memory of the horse and wagon that his father used to drive the five miles to work led him to be interested in driving. Soon the couple had acquired a registered Morgan named Chester, trained for both riding and driving in the show ring. Then they bought a cart, and they were off into sharing an enthusiasm for the sport. Sue wonders now why she didn't ride Chester, supposing that the reason is that she had been told that only experts should ride him, because he was high spirited, and she did not consider herself that good a rider.

Various horses followed, resulting in the later years in the Norwegian Fjord mare named Askepott and the Icelandic mare named Skjona, a small black and white horse with the smooth gait called a tolt. The Fjord was used almost exclusively for driving and the Icelandic for riding, because Sue felt that her smooth gait was easier on her back as well as more pleasant and less tiring than the trot of the Fjord. Sue said, "Skjona was such a great horse for me as she would go anywhere in the area, and I always had the feeling that if I said, 'Let's go swim in the pond,' she would love it."

I asked Sue if she felt completely safe driving instead of riding, because I myself do not, fearing what might happen if the horse became scared and the cart tipped. She said that yes, she did, but then recounted two scary experiences she had had. In the one, she was alone driving on a country road near their property when something scared her horse into galloping off down the hill, only stopping at the pond near the bottom. The other involved her husband also. In completing a circle near their home, they had to go onto Route 122 briefly, a double-laned road from Orange to Petersham. A large gravel truck came along from behind, and all was well until, as it passed, the driver shifted gears. That noise spooked the horse, and off it went, fortunately slowing before turning into the road home.

Sue and Fred decided that the shortcut was not worth the danger and never ventured again onto Route 122.

There were three other important facets in Sue's life besides horses. For twenty-five years she taught as a special needs teacher in Petersham, having gone back to college for her teaching certificate. She became a certified occupational therapist. She says she still misses the daily contact with children. Sue also kept a flock of fifty breeding sheep, which she termed multipurpose, meaning that they were suitable both for their wool and their meat. These were Horned Dorsets and Polled Dorsets to begin with, and later Hampshire, Scottish Blackface, Romney Marsh, and Merino. I asked her what led to that time-consuming occupation, and she responded that she had always wanted to spin and weave. In fact, she opened and ran a yarn shop at her house for many years. I guess the farmer in her genes came to the fore.

Sue continued riding the Icelandic, accompanied by Rob, her beloved Border Collie, until the age of eighty-three. Then everything went downhill. Her husband's health failed, and she nursed him through an extremely difficult year, ending in his death. It was at this point that she gave up riding, partially because she lacked a riding companion. In the past, she would ride out with Rob accompanying her, and then Fred would often meet her at the end of the trail, or at least be at the farm to greet her on her return. With her husband gone and Rob in poor health, riding alone would not have been as safe nor as pleasurable.

Next came the famous December 2008 ice storm, which presented Sue not only with the challenge of surviving herself but with the difficulty of feeding and watering her two horses. Then in the fall of 2009, her faithful but aged Border Collie, Rob, became seriously ill, and she had to face putting him down. Add to this Sue's increasing problem with a spinal situation that leads to occasional severe pain in her legs. She was determined not to lose the ability to walk and is now doing all she can in the way of exercise and therapy to ward off that possibility. Sue knew it was time to find another home for her horses. Fortunately, she was able to do so.

Sue is a pretty, now grandmotherly woman with a ready smile. One might not suspect that she has what is sometimes called guts. Within a few weeks, she sensibly brought into her home the fifth Border Collie of her life, an eight-year-old named Claire, that her breeder (a friend of Sue) declared not very talented in rounding up sheep. When I visited, Claire had been with Sue less than a week, and she was looking forward to training her as she had previous dogs—and above all, having Claire as a companion. I feel sure she will succeed.

*Bill Kingman at 66 on Kilcullen with the Tanheath Hunt in the Southboro area*

# BILL KINGMAN

## Age 79
## Acton

The Kingman residence speaks of gentility, an old-fashioned word that almost asks to be used here. As Bill early on told me, the basic house was built in the mid nineteenth century. On buying it in 1962, he and his wife, Nancy, immediately made necessary repairs and modernizations, including central heating and a drilled well. They furnished it with quiet elegance, befitting the home of a couple who actively participate in one of the two New England fox hunts that still manage to pursue a live fox—the Nashoba Valley Hunt. In fact, Bill for a number of years was fieldmaster and for twenty-five years has been president of that hunt.

Bill grew up in Concord. His sisters had horses, and occasionally Bill would ride the trails, but he was more interested in the usual boys' team sports than in horses. He graduated from Yale University and served in the Navy during the Korean War. In 1961, he entered his father's investment management firm. This became Appleton Partners, Inc., and at his present age of seventy-nine, Bill still spends one day a week at the firm.

And how did this man, clearly not born enamored of horses, get into fox hunting? It started when a friend of his father wanted to retire a Tennessee Walker and gave the horse to Bill, who had space for it on his property. Many of his friends and cohorts fox hunted with the Old Northbridge Hunt, a drag hunt, and they suggested he come along and give it a try. Several members also rode with the Nashoba Valley Hunt, a live hunt, and he soon joined it. He speaks in glowing terms of riding out with the hunt on an early fall morning—the mist, the sound of the horses' hooves on dry leaves, and listening for the hounds to pick up a scent and "give tongue." (For the unitiated, that phrase refers to the various sounds of barking and howling that hounds make to declare they have found a fox scent.)

Although Bill stopped actually riding with the hunt at the age of seventy-one, he continues to go out with them on foot. Some explanation of how the Nashoba Valley Hunt pursues the sport these days in the middle of modern, often densely forested Massachusetts, is necessary here. Fox hunting originated in Europe at a time when the countryside was wide open, foxes abounded, and one field after another offered itself for a good run and a full view of the hounds in action. In sections of the United States, particularly in the south and west, this is sometimes still the situation. But up here in New England, there are problems. In the eastern sections, the prevalence of dangerous roads, where crossing hounds could get killed and where few fox live, has led dedicated fox hunters to turn to drag hunting, in which a bag of fox scent has been dragged over a course that will keep the hounds out of danger but still provide some scenting challenge and the possibility of an interesting chase. Most hunts make use of heavily forested conservation land and wildlife management areas.

The Nashoba Valley Hunt is based near Fitchburg in north central Massachusetts, where the situation requires considerable effort to make possible a live hunt. The hounds chase both foxes and coyotes, the latter being more prevalent and at least as cagey as the fox. The problem, of course, is keeping track of the hounds, who enter thick undergrowth after their prey and consequently completely disappear from the view of the huntsman, who is supposedly keeping them together and urging them to hunt in a sensible and safe direction.

Enter modern technology. A radio collar and / or GPS device is fixed to the collar of one or two of the lead hounds, with signals sent to someone on the ground, who in turn is in radio communication with the huntsman and master. Here is where Bill Kingman comes in, along with others whose vehicles are parked beside sections of roads where hounds might be expected to cross. In other words, an active ground crew, with technological know-how as well as knowledge of the hunt and the territory, is necessary to a live hunt. (Should I mention here that although Bill handles the hunt's technology, he leaves computer work to his wife?)

As Bill explained the extraordinary effort required to run a live hunt, I realized that he was focusing more on hounds than horses, more on the excitement and camaraderie of the hunt than on the skill of the rider. Riding round and round in a ring, he stated clearly, is not for him, nor are long trail rides. His focus has been on hunting, so he would exercise his horse several times a week in the early morning during hunting season to keep him fit and then go to work in Boston.

He gave high praise to any horse with the natural instinct for a hunt. He spoke of his favorite and last mount, Kilcullen, an Irish gelding mix, a big horse and one who knew what was going on in a hunt and loved it. Bill told a story about a time after he had retired as fieldmaster and was following at a slower pace. He said that when he and Cully had stopped, perhaps on a hill, to try to hear the hounds and guess where the fox was going, this horse was mentally way ahead of him. Kilcullen's ears would tell the story of what he could hear and Bill could not, and he was usually correct. Bill relates that one time the horse actually reached his mouth back to Bill's stirrup and grabbed it, his way of saying, "Hey, let's go. This way."

Another hunt-related story is about his Corgi, named Sandy, who a few years ago was sitting with Bill in his Blazer before the hunt and looking out the window. Apparently some teenage girls saw this and insisted that the dog was indeed the fox that was about to be let out so that the hunt could begin. This is a slight illustration of how little most people know in these times about fox hunting! Bill found out about this incident from one of the land owners, who asked if Nashoba was using bagged foxes.

Mainly, though, Bill wanted to talk of hounds. This is also the passion of Daphne Taylor, one of the masters of the Nashoba Valley Hunt. She and her husband Edmund care for, breed, train, and exercise the hunt's hounds—a big job indeed. The excellence of the hounds is the core of hunting for Bill, and hunting is the key to his attachment to horses. He "just loves to watch the hounds work."

In a sport as potentially dangerous and unpredictable as fox hunting, there will be stories of near disaster. One that Bill told is of a hunt where he personally was not as closely familiar with the landscape as he is in other areas. He was riding a new horse, not as reliable as Kilcullen, when they galloped through a field and up a hill, only to be surprised by a steep downhill on the other side. He managed to pull his horse in, but he was bumped by the horse behind him, and his horse fell down onto his knees. Apparently several horses behind this pair also dumped their riders, because when Daphne rode back to help, she afterward laughingly said that "there was a sea of red coats all over the field."

That remark by Daphne, the moving spirit of the hunt, is a slight indication of the camaraderie of this group of people. Stories are told at the breakfasts that follow their long and exhausting hunts. Bill mentioned another incident that occurred to a Nashoba master named John Quincy Adams, a descendant of the original. At a brook crossing, he happened to lose his hunting cap, which amusingly filled with water and kept floating down the brook, difficult for a mounted man to retrieve and a situation of amusement to the the field, a member of which returned the hat.

Still another time, when hunting in the Lake Dennison area in the snow, as Cully rose up to jump a log, the huntsman right ahead of him knocked against a branch laden **with** snow, and both Bill and Cully emerged completely white. There is a yearly award for the individual who makes the biggest mistake during a hunting season. Bill says he has received it a few times and that it is a chamber pot to be prominently displayed throughout the next hunting season. The last time Bill was chosen to receive it, his wife Nancy placed a potted amaryllis in it. A special bond develops within such a group.

*Bill at 45 on Cuthbert in 1976 in Pepperell, with his wife Nancy on Comnac Ronan*

I think this bond, as well as Bill's continued participation in the hunt as a non-rider, made his decision to stop riding less difficult than it can be for many of us. When his talented horse Kilcullen had to be put down, he tried using his daughter's horse Spinaker for one season, but it wasn't the same. He really did not look forward to fussing with a new horse—not at the age of seventy-one and with difficulties starting to appear in his knees. His wife felt it was time for him to stop riding and not take a chance with his health. He agreed, and although Bill says he still misses the whinny of the early morning greeting, he

111

never regretted no longer having to expend the effort required to care for horses year round.

So now Bill retains everything that he has most loved: watching hounds work on early fall mornings, helping to track them, recounting stories and developing fresh ones with new and old friends, and doing his best to ensure that live fox hunting with excellent hounds continues somewhere in New England. Who needs to ride a horse? Who needs to care for a horse during a blizzard? He still has what is the best of it for him, because "the hounds are everything"!

*Beverly Murphy at 56 riding Tick Tock at a*
*Stoney-B horse show in 1979*

# BEVERLY MURPHY

## Age 87
## Greenfield

I was particularly delighted to have unearthed Beverly Murphy. I see her as representing the millions of women infected with the incurable horse-loving virus but whom the New England horse community, viewed as the multiple equestrian associations throughout the area, rarely has reason to notice. For twenty-seven years, Beverly was a salesperson at Wilson's department store in Greenfield. She learned to ride at a local stable, kept the horse she owned at that stable, took her children to that stable to learn to ride, and when she ventured elsewhere it was to commercial dude ranches in other states. No equestrian meetings, no participation in equestrian events beyond her stable—just riding for the love of horses.

Like many of her time, Beverly had access to horses early in her life, because her grandparents owned Apple Valley, a farm in Buckland. She enjoyed visiting there from her home in Greenfield, loving not only the horses but the cows and calves. She told me of the thrill of being asked to back one of the draft horses out of his stall—she was so little and he so big. Not that there were no horses in the town of Greenfield in that era. Her uncle owned a horse named Brownie who apparently had access to several back yards on Conway Street. He would be hitched to sleds in the winter. Beverly remembers one hot summer day when, to rescue Brownie from the heat, she brought him up the four or five steps onto the porch of a house and then was unable to entice him to go down, having to call her father to help. This same horse also allowed a dog to ride on his back. The children of the neighborhood must have had a ball with him.

Horses were not Beverly's only passion—roller skating was the other. The Gables in South Deerfield had a wonderful roller skating rink where she went three times a week. Here she met her future husband, Bill, and together they won a "Waltzing on Skates" trophy as the most graceful couple. They had a chance to skate professionally, but World War II interfered. Beverly and Bill were married during the war, and the marriage lasted sixty-four years until his death in 2007.

After she married and had children, Beverly herself had few opportunities for riding although she did manage to ride occasionally in Montague. Finally she discovered Verne Gilette in Gill, who had seventeen horses and would take riders out onto nearby trails—no riding lessons, just out you would go and hope to stay on. She and others often went out riding with Verne for several years. She laughed remembering one time when she and he were entering a field and he mysteriously told her to ride across slowly to the gate on the other side. When he rode over afterwards, he quickly opened the gate so both could pass through it, mentioning that there was a bull in the field they had just crossed. Eventually, Verne had a serious fall and sold his horses.

Shortly thereafter, Beverly connected with Valerie Dean, who became her most important horse contact and good friend. Valerie managed (and still does) Stoney-B Acres in Bernardston, and here Beverly took lessons for many years, also riding the considerable trails behind the stable. She bought Cherokee, a chestnut Quarter Horse mare, keeping her with Valerie and riding about three times a week. When her grandson Sean came to live with her, Beverly took him for lessons with Valerie, and he participated in the 4-H activities at that stable.

Like anyone who has ridden for years, Beverly has stories of disaster or near disaster. She tells that as she and Cherokee were returning to Val's stable one day, two horses broke loose from behind a fence and followed them. The owners caught them, but they got out again when she passed close to the other side of the pasture and actually followed Beverly all the way to the stable. Val saw them coming and yelled, "Get off! Get off!" and then took care of the situation. Still another time, when trying a new trail with a friend, her horse spooked. Beverly started to fall, and she says when she found herself "looking into the horse's eye," she dropped off, resulting in a broken arm.

The stable was not always a place of rural contentment and peace. In addition to about thirty horses, there were pigs, ducks, chickens, goats, and geese. Beverly tells a story about those geese. Cherokee, a mare, was out in a pasture with a gelding, and perhaps she was in heat. (Beverly said she "didn't know about such things.") At any rate, the mare would not come, so someone suggested she get some grain to attract her. When Beverly went into the grain shed, she found herself followed by Rusty, a large goat who clearly wanted to come in and get some grain. Children could ride on Rusty's back. He loved to be groomed and seemed to believe he was a horse. At this time, however, Rusty decided that he definitely was going to get hold of Beverly's grain and kept her penned in the grain room for a long time. Finally she reached over the door and hit him with a boot, solving the situation.

Another incident involved a gander who attacked her legs, flapping his wings and attacking again and again. Fortunately, Whitey Streeter happened to arrive, grabbed the gander, threw him into a stall, and later disappeared with him. Whitey (whose sketch appears earlier in this section) was the animal control officer of Bernardston, so we can guess the end of the story.

Eventually, Cherokee went blind in one eye and started shying from puddles and such. She had to be put down and was buried on a hill at Stoney-B. Of course, Beverly found this extremely difficult. After Cherokee died, she acquired another horse for grandson Sean, a large strawberry gelding named Cinnamon. Her husband Bill and she would announce at shows and "work the ribbons" at Stoney-B Acres for Valerie, a task that only last year she undertook again, her husband having died two years ago. Referring to her helping at Stoney-B, Beverly said "I loved every minute of it."

Vacations involved either trips to the ocean or riding. Beverly and her husband went twice a year to a rustic dude ranch in Downsville, New York, a mountainous area. While Bill played golf, she would ride—morning, noon, and evening. She helped round up horses, and groups of riders would play a "Cowboy and Indian" game, which apparently consisted of one group hiding and then suddenly surprising another group as it came along. (This sounds to me like a recipe for disaster!) There was dancing in the evening, and the couples soon made friends and looked forward to seeing each other again on subsequent visits. Beverly also recounted another vacation riding experience when she was visiting her daughter and grandchildren in Montana. She and a friend went horseback riding with two cowboys in the Badlands, and they ran into a herd of wild horses. "What a great experience," said Beverly.

She gradually stopped riding at the age of seventy-five on doctor's orders. He said that the bouncing would affect the pacemaker that she required. (It seems that all doctors who don't ride horseback are under the illusion that even a good rider bounces.) It is surprising that she did not quit earlier for other reasons. A diabetic, she also has rheumatoid arthritis, which made mounting difficult. "Did it hurt when you were actually riding?" I asked. "No," she responded. "Then I had a smile on my face." She said that she "found great peace and enjoyment at Stoney-B with all the horses, other animals, and friends."

Beverly volunteered that there are two experiences she still wants to repeat: She wants to see the ocean again, and she wants to sit on the back of a horse once more. Valerie Dean has offered to make the latter possible anytime.

*Marcy Gamester at 70 on Moon*

# MARCY GAMESTER
## Age 71
## Westford

ECTRA (Eastern Competitive Trail Riders Association) records a total of more than eleven thousand miles during thirty-one years of competitive trail riding for Marcy Gamester, a small, very active, and fit seventy-one-year-old woman. She remains among the top ten long-distance riders on the East Coast. She also has accumulated four thousand miles of pleasure riding, including five hundred miles in 2009. One wonders if she has had time to do anything else!

In fact, she has done many other things. She raised three boys, for twenty-two years held down a job at Raytheon, and ran a stable that has grown from a backyard business to a present total of sixteen horses, three of which are Marcy's—Max, Moon Unit, and Shaakan. Although not raised with horses, as a child she did get to play with farm kids and join a 4-H club. Marcy knew as a young woman that she wanted horses in her life, telling her husband-to-be very early that horses were a part of the deal. Although not a rider himself, husband Richard is comfortable handling horses and has been wonderfully supportive, not only in backing her stable enterprise, but in regularly accompanying her on weekend riding adventures. He has driven the van, set up the overnight camp, done the barbecuing, and actively enjoyed the camaraderie of the competitive riders. He is viewed as a treasure and a rarity by the mostly female, serious competitive riders.

Marcy graduated as an animal technician from Holliston Junior College at the age of forty and prepared to take her internship. However, just as she was beginning, a problem with her mare led to a fall that popped Marcy's hip out—back, not forward as is apparently usual. For a long time, she was on crutches, an unacceptable situation for her supervisor. Needing employment, Marcy got a job at Raytheon that paid better and kept her in horses for many years.

Marcy has enjoyed her stable business. For twelve years, a 4-H club was based at her place, and she would teach elementary riding to women in the mornings and to kids in the afternoons. Now her boarders (a word commonly used to refer both to owners and horses) by and large come and stay, and many have become longtime friends. She is a very attentive and knowledgable horsewoman. She feeds grain and hay three times a day, at the potentially inconvenient hours of eight, three, and eight. Although she allows boarders some leeway in feed, she has instituted an overall system with certain requirements, such as vitamin E and selenium. Each horse has its own run-in stall and paddock with no horses put out together.

Marcy's boarders have been like a family to her, taking over the chores when she and her husband go away weekends on competitive trail rides. In return, she obviously cares about them all and helps them with their problems, both horse-related and others. Marcy said, not joking, "I get women who come here, have had them as kids, they marry, divorce after twenty years, and say they would rather have the horse than the husband." She continued in this vein concerning a woman who wanted to bring her horse to the stable and mentioned that she was divorced. Marcy responded "That's good, so we won't have to go through the divorce with you."

As Marcy spoke with me about the various horses she has owned and competed, I was struck by the fact that these were not obvious animals to choose for a competitive sport. None seemed to be a strong, laid-back, ready-to-ride horse. First there was a three-quarters Arabian gelding familiarly called Shake. Born as a liver chestnut, he became rose gray, dapple gray, and eventually white. He was the first horse to do both five thousand and six thousand miles in ECTRA. However, as a four-year-old, he contracted chronic obstructive pulmonary disease (COPD), an incurable bronchial condition often referred to as heaves. Not an obvious candidate for long rides. During the twenty-two years that Shake lived, Marcy administered medication, consulted veterinarians, provided moist hay, and made various adjustments to her horse trailer so that Shake would not be subjected to dust. She finally took him to Dr. Stuart Harvey in Palmer, apparently a famous, knowledgable, but somewhat intimidating old veterinarian, whom "one did not question." And Marcy says she did not question him, despite his seemingly odd regimen for the horse. Regardless of all that, Shake kept winning and adding on miles.

Then there was Max, a chestnut Egyptian Arabian, an "Anchor Hill horse," which apparently made him very special. When Marcy acquired him at the age of fourteen for minimal payment of his previous owner's unpaid board, he was a handful. He was afraid of being put outside and would settle down only in a small, confined area. Max was a professionally trained show horse but had been kept in tiny quarters. Marcy sensibly decided to sell him. And then, "after five weeks of hell" with the gelding, Max put his head on her shoulder. Of course, she kept him, somehow managed to ride and compete him, and he is now twenty-seven years old and still in her barn.

Another not-obvious winner was Gazon, a gray full Arabian that Marcy rode for nine years and more than two thousand miles. This horse would allow cars to open the farm gate and drive through, but he forbade them to leave, becoming obnoxious when they attempted. Nor was he easy for Marcy to handle, unmounted or mounted. However, one day she found a young friend Patti, whom she had warned about Gazon, riding him happily with only a snaffle bit. Eventually, as this strange friendship between horse and rider continued, Marcy decided to give Gazon to Patti and be done with the problem.

And now there is Moon Unit, a sixteen-year-old bay gelding Morab she has had since he was seven months old. A twin, he had to be bottle-fed, which Marcy considers to be one reason he "believes he is equal to the human." He is "cocky," and Marcy says he still challenges her, but she loves the way he wants to move out on trail rides. Moon Unit has done a thousand miles of competitive and three thousand miles of pleasure riding, including five hundred miles this past year. Recently, Marcy was notified that this horse (officially named Travelon's Times Two) has accumulated more than six thousand points and will be listed in the International Morab Association Hall of Fame. Marcy said it took her eleven years to accomplish this feat with Moon Unit.

About the parade of difficult horses she has owned, Marcy remarked: "There are a few bad apples out there, but as far as I'm concerned, many can be straightened out. I have taken in many horses that people have given up on. I get them free and work with them until they are safe. Sometimes it takes me a few years, and if I can't use them myself, I find a person suited for that horse."

The process of dealing with such horses began when Marcy was in her teens. When she was only twelve or thirteen, at a riding stable, she was entrusted to take out a trail ride, and as the group approached a gully leading onto a road, they encountered a parked car right at the top. Her horse, surprised, ran straight into the car, of course dumping young Marcy, who appeared so injured and covered in blood that she was thought dead. Her companions decided to cover her head with a blanket. In a while she moved, finally getting up and leading her horse back to the farm, where her injuries were only discovered somewhat later and she was taken to the hospital. Since that early experience, she has broken her pelvis and hurt this and that along the way, but none of these injuries apparently has discouraged her from riding.

Another unfortunate experience for Marcy when she was a teenager occurred with the first horse that she actually owned, a gangly black-and-white spotted gelding named Randy Run, bought from a summer horse camp for girls. She worked hard with him for ten days and showed him locally on a Saturday. On Sunday he became sick, and on Monday the decision was made to put him down. Marcy recalled to me in detail what happened and how she felt. "I heard the killer's truck back down the driveway. My heart was pounding. The rattling of the chain was eerie, and when the gun went off, I felt the shot pierce my heart. Yes, I finally had my own horse, such a beauty. I had ten days of happiness, and it ended with a single shot. I never wanted to own another horse again."

But of course she recovered and in fact owned another one soon after. That was Blacky, who was scrawny to begin with, but once he fattened up, he became a runaway. Then followed Sugar, a 14.2-hand, pure white, blue-eyed horse who kept on running back to the farm from which he was acquired, and when ridden would rear, spin, and back into trees. She finally fell from this horse, caught her foot in the stirrup, and was dragged. The odd ending is that Sugar was the first of Marcy's Champions.

With the various horses Marcy has owned and boarded, it is not surprising that her body has had to put up with a few falls. I asked Marcy, now that she is seventy-one years old, if she has changed any of her riding practices over the last few years, and she said that no, she really hasn't. She might ask her husband to handle a very strong horse on the ground, but that was it. And she has decided to forego competitive trail riding while continuing with pleasure rides. She had grown tired of all the standing around at competitive trail rides, as horses were examined one by one for blood pressure and heartbeat. Understandable, after thirty-one years of doing so.

Meanwhile, Marcy is involved with fifteen riding organizations. She is treasurer for two and on the board of one. Among these organizations are the local Littleton Horse Owner Association and the New England Horse and Trail Association, both of which run trail rides. Two of her horses, Moon Unit and Max, are certified with the Mounted Search & Rescue associated with the Massachusetts State Police, and then there is the Arabian Horse Association of Massachusetts to which she has belonged for years.

Marcy will obviously continue to be a familiar presence at most of the pleasure trail rides in New England for a long, long time.

*Dorothy McFarland at 69 on her Thoroughbred-Morgan cross, Moo Mare, outside Xenophon Farm*

# DOROTHY McFARLAND

## Age 71
## Leverett

Some lives seem to unfold in distinct phases, related one to the other but in ways that are discernible only in looking back. As Dorothy McFarland, now seventy-one, told me the story of her horse-related life so far, the interconnectedness and development of her skills and interests began to form a pattern.

Dorothy was one of those little girls who, like me and many others, always loved horses and wanted to ride, but did not have a horse-loving parent to whom satisfying this desire made practical sense. She dates awareness of her passion to a day when at the age of seven she watched two draft horses being used to excavate a basement and fell permanently in love with the entire species. Without real horses to ride, she filled her mind with imaginary ones, drawing horses, playing horse games, and reading horse books, but that did little to assuage her passion.

At the age of ten, Dorothy had a friend whose mother, a competent rider, one day took her daughter and Dorothy to a nearby stable and out onto a trail for their first walk, trot, and canter experience. Heaven. The following year, Dorothy was in luck when her Girl Scout troop voted to earn a horseback riding badge. A nearby stable offered a bargain rate—ten lessons for ten dollars. The lessons were elementary and basically Western, although she did learn to post English-style.

Skip about fifteen years during which she achieved a bachelor's degree in English from the University of California at Berkeley and her master's in comparative literature from Columbia University. At the age of twenty-six, she married and moved to Leverett—horse country, with horses here, there, and everywhere. Her husband was teaching at the University of Massachusetts at Amherst, in effect just down the road, and it so happened that the wife of the president of UMass was a horsewoman who welcomed trail riding companions.

Dorothy managed to meet her and was invited to ride with her on Morgan horses owned by the university. Soon she discovered that Mount Holyoke had horses and offered lessons to the public. She took some lessons there from one of those taskmasters that I have noted are so often hired for such purposes, and she would come home in tears, feeling as if she just could not ride at all. But back she would go again.

Finally, at the age of thirty, Dorothy took riding lessons at UMass, where she rode for a few years, doing some jumping. Unfortunately in 1979, her sacroiliac joint went out when the horse she was riding paused a split second before taking a jump. The small jolt was all it took to destabilize a weak area, and her back went into chronic spasm, making it impossible for her to ride for seven years. During this period, Dorothy was teaching yoga in the physical education department at UMass and writing short books and encyclopedia articles on various authors in contemporary literature for the New York publisher Frederick Ungar.

Dorothy had not forgotten how wonderful it could feel to ride, and she began to imagine how it would feel to be on the back of a horse. This imagining made her suspect that just maybe it would be possible for her to begin riding again. Enter Xenophon Stables, just six miles away. Driving past this facility, she began to think of trying to ride again, because she had always been interested in dressage and the name Xenophon suggested classical horsemanship instruction. So Dorothy began to ride under the instruction of the owner and trainer, Janice Kachavos, entering what for her was a new and wonderful world, dressage riding. Much to her surprise, she found that riding strengthened her legs and helped loosen her back. She began weekly lessons on various horses, but she particularly liked Eagle, a leopard Appaloosa owned by a weekend rider.

Two years later, at the age of fifty-one and after she had completed her last book contract, Dorothy bought Eagle and began a regime of daily riding. She and Eagle learned dressage together, competing in training levels 1 through 4. She kept him stabled at Xenophon Farm and worked on dressage with him for seventeen years. He eventually became blind and developed Cushing's disease. For a while, his lack of vision upset him, but he apparently became accustomed to it, and at one event at Xenophon he won a walk-trot competition when completely blind. When his condition worsened, he was put down, but not until the age of thirty-four.

After Eagle's death, Dorothy was given Moo by friend Ami Weber. The full name of this Thoroughbred-Morgan cross is Moo Mare, an odd name for any horse, much less a 16-hand bay mare. It turns out that the first owner had a little girl familiar with cows but not horses. She was the source of the name, which Dorothy has shortened to Moo. Ami had competed Moo in cross country events. Moo loved to jump, but when at the age of seventeen she developed difficulties with her right front foot, Amy knew she ought to retire her from cross country jumping .

Dorothy has owned Moo for only three years and amusingly terms her "rather a freight train." Janice and Dorothy immediately began Moo's dressage training and worked together for two years, competing her through training level 3. And then life dramatically changed for Dorothy. As she was leading Moo through a complex system of gates and ropes in the paddocks, the mare became frightened and spooked, going upwards and sideways, knocking Dorothy high into the air. She says it was high enough to give her time to wish she knew more about how to land. And the landing was bad, breaking the trochanter in Dorothy's left leg. Surgery was required. Nerve damage developed, and after sixteen months Dorothy is still at times using a cane to relieve the weight on that leg.

Seven months after the accident, however, she returned to riding. It was a matter of figuring out who could help her and being willing to accept that help. Her husband often goes with her to the arena to bring Moo into the paddock, and she calls him a "groom-in-training." Dorothy says she can put on the saddle, but then when she tries to mount, her left leg can't bear the weight. Not to be stopped, she has devised a very high mounting block that puts her left foot at the height of the stirrup, so that all she has to do is support herself enough to slip over the horse. This block consists of a low wooden mounting block already available at the stable plus a three-tier commercial mounting block. Moo stands still at mounting. Once on board, Dorothy found that riding is an excellent therapy, both physically and mentally. The horse's movement helps her to free up her hips, making walking more comfortable. She said that the intense mental focus and the feeling of communication with her horse always lift her spirits.

Dorothy rides now for a half hour four times a week. On two of those days, Janice schools Moo for a half hour and then gives Dorothy a lesson for a half hour. Dorothy delights in what she is doing and feels that without the left leg muscle working, she is speaking more to the horse through her weight and is riding better. She finds working on dressage with Moo "endlessly engrossing." And the horse is improving, having started at T-2 and now working on T-4, terms that meant nothing to me, so I asked her to give me a short course in what dressage riding involves, and she enthusiastically complied.

As I listened, I realized that learning dressage is like learning to communicate in a new, complex, and subtle language, the language of the body. The rider must understand and sense both what her own body is telling the horse and also what the horse's body is telling her. The rider must have some understanding of how both bodies work. As a writer, language was Dorothy's trade; as a yoga teacher, the human body and mind interested her; and as a horse lover, the equine body and mind fascinated her. While a horse has strong herd instincts and as a prey animal instinctively flees when frightened, a human has lesser versions of both. We need to socialize with each other and we sometimes flee, but we also enjoy solitude and have predatory instincts. We share enough of his basics instincts to understand the horse.

Not long after Dorothy, at the age of fifty-one, bought Eagle, she found a body worker who helped her learn to release the holding patterns in her back muscles that still lingered after her earlier injury. Within a few years she adapted those techniques and began doing what she terms "therapeutic body work" on other people. She explained that this is a hands-on technique for releasing unconscious patterns of muscle contraction. Had she ever gone into such work with a horse's body? She said she had done a bit of this, but that her hands were more talented on the human body. Dorothy practiced this therapeutic body work full-time for about ten years, with more clients than she really had time for. She has a sensitivity for and an intellectual interest in the intricacies of the body and its means of communication. In dressage, the horse is added to the human.

From literature studies, Dorothy had proceeded to nonfiction writing primarily about literature, which is of course a way that human beings communicate, and then on to learning how horses communicate, their language. From yoga, she had expanded to therapeutic body work and then applied her talent to the movements of horse and rider in dressage. Both streams (communication methods and the intricacies of body movement) gradually converged for her in dressage.

At seventy-one, after twenty years with dressage, she is still excited about moving ahead with the discipline. When asked about curtailing her riding as she ages, she says that, of course, after her injuries she is more afraid of falling off, but that she leaves behind any fear once she is mounted. She remains "totally engaged" with dressage riding. It is clear that stopping riding is not something she bothers to think about.

*Molly Scott at 71 with her Paso Fino, Mahka*

# MOLLY SCOTT

## Age 72
## Charlemont

Molly Scott learned to ride at the best age and in the best way possible—as a very young child and with an ornery pony. She was raised in a small New York town where her family had several horses, some gaited. During her teens and twenties, although away from home, she contrived to ride here and there, whenever and wherever she could. Horses were never far from her mind.

After graduating from Smith College in 1959, Molly became part of the early folk music revival of the sixties, performing on the West Coast and in New York City. She was also active in theater and television, even for a time hosting her own television show on CBS. In the seventies, she moved up to Western Massachusetts with her family, started a musical group called Sumitra, and used her talents to support peace and environmental causes, which she still does. She has performed with the Mohawk Trail Concerts, with the Springfield Symphony, and at the Iron Music Hall as well as for numerous local benefits. And somewhere along the line she earned her master's and doctoral degrees at the University of Massachusetts in Amherst. She also is an LMHC (Licensed Mental Health Counselor) and has founded the Creative Resonance Institute, which integrates voice use with psychotherapy. She now has her own private psychotherapy practice in Shelburne Falls.

As a singer, psychotherapist, and poet, Molly sounds a bit intimidating, especially when one sees added to her name Ed.D as well as the LMHC or when one accesses more information about her from the web. However, the words that come to mind when one meets Molly in her home are more like welcoming, enthusiastic, warm, open. Her distinguished background remains in the background.

135

Molly lives by herself on a three hundred-acre property atop Route 8A in Charlemont. She acquired this heavily forested property in 1967 and built her house in 1974. Owning horses then became a possibility. Probability? Necessity. Even after becoming a horse owner, she has managed to ride wherever she goes, including Iceland, Denmark, India, and Costa Rica. Riding an unfamiliar horse in unfamiliar settings apparently doesn't faze her in the least.

In recent years, she has found ways to combine her understanding of horses with her psychotherapy interest. She is a certified professional with the Equine Assisted Growth and Learning Association (EAGALA), which is "dedicated to improving the mental health of individuals, families, and groups around the world by setting the standard of excellence in equine-assisted psychotherapy." Molly and several colleagues run workshops that provide "the opportunity to explore the rich potential for a spirit-soul relationship with horses."

An interesting example of her combining horses with psychotherapy is the horse labyrinth that she has created on her own property. This is an area laid out in rocks in a seven-branch pattern, forty feet across, with sharp turns designed for walking horses in-hand. Its purpose in general terms is to develop concentration, to facilitate meditation, and to deepen spirituality. Although her horse labyrinth was Molly's own inspiration, she has discovered that such patterns exist in other countries. She also runs the Alternate Healthcare Clinic, which uses horses for mental disability therapy.

Molly is a lover of gaited horses, but she has owned others as well. She spoke most of Shanti, a bay Morab who lived to be twenty-six years old, and a blue roan registered Tennessee Walker mare named Tillie. Presently she owns a Paso Fino mix named Mahka (mother earth in the Lakota language), a small fourteen-year-old buckskin mare, and recently a gray twelve-

*Molly's horse labyrinth from the air and Mahka and Riley grazing there*

year-old Arabian gelding named Riley, mostly as a companion for Mahka. For Molly, Mahka has been the perfect trail horse, eager to go, willing, not easily scared. Also, she has found that the side-to-side motion of one's hips on a gaited horse, as contrasted with the back-and-forth on a trotting horse, has helped relieve her various back problems and increased her bone density. Although Molly does ride alone—and more of that later—she doesn't currently find as much time as she would like to take off on the trails with Mahka. When she does, she says it may be for four or five hours.

Molly jokes that she "got Mahka for a song," which is just about literally true. A few years ago, she stopped for a bite to eat in Bernardston at a small restaurant since replaced by a bakery. She was sitting quietly at an outside table, so far minding her own business, when an exuberant group of obvious horse people settled at another table, where they started to celebrate a member's birthday. With the usual song, of course. Molly couldn't resist, so raised her voice with the rest. And then joined the group. One of the guys let drop that he was trying to sell his Paso Fino, because he just couldn't adjust to the gait. Molly's ears perked up—a gaited horse. After a few more songs, she arranged to meet the horse, rode her, loved her, and got her "for a song." Molly described her pleasure in the horse by saying, "the gaits of my little horse are the *sine qua non* of horse dance." Mounted on beloved Mahka, moving in the inimitable Paso Fino four-beat lateral gait, she "feels like a centaur."

When I asked about her best and worst experiences with horses, Molly dismissed a time in 1999 when she was dumped during a bad shy and broke a bunch of ribs. That was only physical pain. For a worst experience, she settled on the long and harrowing death of her beloved thirty-one-year-old Tillie from colic.

As for best experiences, Molly told about her horseback rides five or six years ago on the Osa Peninsula in Costa Rica, described by the *National Geographic* as "the most biologically intense place on earth." She was co-leader of a group of twenty-two who traveled there for a workshop with this highly descriptive (but mighty long) title: Come to the Garden: Tuning into Peace in Costa Rica with Breath, Voice, and the Deep Wisdom of Nature. The ride that was billed as "an easy ramble along the beach" turned out to be what Molly described as "a challenging inland journey over rough terrain, fording horse-belly high rivers, and scrambling up narrow clay banks with treacherous footing." All this during three or four hours in the hot tropical sun. Although the pace had to be slow, there was sufficient challenge for Molly to find it thrilling.

Horses are integral to who Molly is. She said that they "are a part of my wiring." They connect her "with her inner self and with the land." She explains that riding expands her feeling of life. Her almost mystical identification with her horse, feeling "like a centaur," is added to her love of the woods through which she rides. She described an opportunity she had to ride bareback into a fresh water pond, saying that the undulating motion of the horse on entering deep water and beginning to swim made her feel "like a dolphin."

Molly seems to be a person who is very awake spiritually regarding just about everything. The poem quoted at the end of this sketch is evidence of this, as are her songs, her style of singing, her work using the voice in trauma therapy, even the pictures and artifacts in her house. Horses are "a heart thing" for her, making possible a "joining" experience with her horse. The concept of being one with the horse, prevalent in riding instruction, takes on new and much deeper meaning.

Feeling one with our horse is great. It is when we are no longer one—in other words, when we take a fall from our horse—that our feeling may at least temporarily change. All riders fall at one time or another. Molly has had her share of those experiences, and in fact quite recently, when riding alone, as she frequently does, not having a ready riding companion. We all know how that is, and sometimes we pay the price—as did Molly this past fall, 2009.

She seems to blame herself as much as Mahka. She admits that she was emotionally upset and had little sleep before she set out on the horse in hopes that the ride would settle her, bring her some peace. She feels that she transmitted her psychological condition to her horse, who felt jumpy beneath her as they started out. Down the road, she saw that a little group of mailboxes had recently been enclosed in a cute little mailbox house. All was well until Mahka belatedly caught sight of it with her eye as they passed, swung round, and headed at a fast gallop for home. Molly lost her stirrups, could not stop the horse, and swung down from the horse's neck, hitting the back of her head hard as she landed. She was wearing a helmet, thank goodness. And Mahka disappeared in the distance. Molly managed somehow to get to her feet and up the steps of a neighbor's house, where she called for help. Only days later did she discover that her main injury was a broken fibula. So much for riding alone.

Few of the songs Molly has written are about horses, but horses do appear in her poetry. One of her poems should be read aloud slowly, listening to the rhythms.

### Horse Dreams

(on looking into her amber eye)

Is it to break my fragile fencing,
breaching the ancient code between us, that she dreams?
Does she, as I do, gallop weightless, winged
over cloud mountains, leaping waves of wind?
At night, when anchored through those tensile legs to ground
does she fly free or is this
my dream for her, to be released from that dense body
and from me?

Even to ask these questions feels like grace
I want to be within her breathing dreams
glued to her shining envelope,
a letter leaping into
God

This is not the poetry of a woman about to stop riding and caring for horses before she becomes physically unable to do so, probably years and years from now.

*Robert Bryant at 66 in Grafton, New York, in 2001*

# ROBERTA BRYANT

## Age 74
### Leverett

When I first saw Roberta Bryant crossing a path at the end of one barn, I did not recognize her as the seventy-four-year-old owner of the Mount Toby Stables at the Craig Memorial Equestrian Center. Her quick and easy way of walking suggested she was one of the young helpers so necessary at a barn of thirty-four horses.

Roberta seems to have fallen into her professional life with horses simply by chance. As a child she enjoyed pony rides at Forest Park in Springfield, but she was not horse crazy. In her teen years, when she had the opportunity to ride, she wanted a "horse that knows how to run." A life full of horses, however, was many years away.

At the age of five, she started working at her father's greenhouse in Agawam, where he grew annuals, perennials, and vegetable plants to sell. She began by filling flats with soil and packing them down. When she was eleven, the family moved the greenhouse piece by piece to Leverett, and she worked there until her dad died in 1967. She ran the greenhouse for the next few years along with caring for the horses she had by that time acquired, eventually giving up the greenhouse.

Roberta was also working in her in-laws' nursing home, at first in the laundry, and then she bought the property and turned it into a rest home in 1967. She owned this establishment and ran it for thirty-nine years, finally selling it to her youngest daughter but still helping out until 2006. Only since that year has she been able to devote herself full-time to horses.

Cut back a few years. After she married, Roberta and her husband set about building a house on a small piece of property in Greenfield in 1957. It wasn't until she had become the mother of three daughters and one son that she finally got a first horse for their sixteen-year-old daughter and then a Welsh Cob for the second daughter, until they had acquired four horses. They then built a house in Leverett, where Roberta and her husband still live. At this point, Roberta was thirty-four years old and not much of a rider beyond being able to stay on—a good start, of course.

Frank Dearborn then entered her life and changed it drastically. He owned a small farm near Leverett Center where he offered trail rides, gave riding lessons, and sold horses. He convinced Roberta and her husband to enter the horse-selling business and sold them no fewer than eighteen untrained horses from out West. They were able to manage by renting out a small building to four boys in exchange for help with the farm work. Sensibly, Roberta finally started riding lessons at Mount Toby Stables. Virginia Goodyear gave lessons to her and her three daughters.

A next major step was Roberta's decision to specialize in Morab horses, which she has done ever since. She has been very active over the years in the several Morab registry associations as they developed and combined, and she breeds Morabs. She now has three stallions. She sells the geldings, preferring to keep the mares for breeding.

The Mount Toby Stables offers everything equestrian in addition to breeding and selling horses. Currently, Roberta boards twenty horses and owns fourteen. She gives riding lessons, with three other licensed instructors. Trail riding is also available, with instruction, on the ample trails toward Mount Toby. Most importantly, local 4-H activities are based at her stables, and as is usual with large stables, she gets a lot of the everyday help required for horses from the pool of young girls wanting to exchange work for riding or board. She really enjoys the children and says that "this relationship with the 4-H club is huge."

The stable's horses regularly appear at parades throughout the region. Roberta tells of several amusing incidents. One occurred at the bottom of Main Street in Greenfield near the present Dunkin' Donuts store and, importantly, the train tracks. As a safety precaution, Roberta usually walks beside her horses rather than riding, and this time her presence on the ground was a lifesaver. A train arrived just as the horses were turning the corner, and of course it blew its whistle. As a few of the horses began to panic, she grabbed the bridle of the lead horse and the rest eventually calmed down. Another time, in a Turners Falls parade, the sudden noise of snare drums surprised and upset the horses, and Roberta was glad once again to have been on foot so she could settle them quickly.

*Roberta at 51 with Pepper sporting a sixth-place ribbon from a forty-mile Woodstock, Vermont, competitive trail ride in 1986*

Roberta lives and breathes horses morning, noon, and night, a necessity for her business. Fortunately, she does still enjoy riding when she gets the opportunity. Competitive trail riding has been her favorite form of the sport for the past twenty-five years. She has done some hundred-mile trail rides with her Morab named Glory, who unfortunately died four years ago at the age of twenty-six. She now rides Glory's daughters but does not find them as reliable as their mother. She also simply hasn't the time to do the daily exercise and training necessary for a horse to compete well over long distances. Roberta misses the companionship of the long rides but has kept her hand into the sport through filling one of the many volunteer spots needed for both competitive and endurance trail rides. Some of these rides have left from her stable.

Roberta seems to thrive on hard work, ascribing her good physical condition and energy to being "on the go" all day. She does have a bone spur in her back, for which she does the appropriate exercises, but otherwise she says she is fine. When asked what changes she has made as she has gotten older, she said that she does not ride the young horses as much as she used to, generally confining her training for them to ground work. Also, she no longer goes out riding the trails by herself, laughing at the way she used to take long midnight rides alone when she was younger. We agreed that at any age that is not safe, but that common sense sometimes is a latecomer for horse enthusiasts, who would not be riding at all if they were not willing to take risks. Roberta is taking the obvious sensible steps to prolong her days of riding.

*Judy Smith at 46 on her Morgan, Nifty, at the Morgan Dressage Competition*

# JUDY SMITH

### Age 77
### Fitchburg

Judy is slender, blue-eyed, friendly. The word that came to mind when I met her was "soignée," defined in one dictionary as "elegantly maintained." At seventy-seven, she has rather short gray hair, wavy, and in place. She does not look like one's idea of a lifetime horsewoman, which is what she most definitely is.

As I entered her home, I was greeted by two beautiful but aging Golden Retrievers, Shannon and Mischief. I discovered that not only have horses been important in Judy's life, but that she has been breeding dogs for a number of years, first Collies and then Golden Retrievers. She spoke warmly of the wonderful families she has met and of the importance of her dogs for their love and companionship.

If I personally could go back eighty years and wish myself a career, I would choose the one that Judy has lived. To my mind, she has done it all. While teaching English in various schools, she has raised five children who have in turn given her thirteen grandchildren and two great granddaughters, owned and ridden zillions of quality horses, managed a twenty-five-acre farm called Smithfield Stables, taught riding to young people of many nationalities, run a summer day camp, headed a 4-H club with sixty members, trained horses in dressage, worked others to high levels in endurance riding, bred Morgans and other breeds, and ridden over hill and dale with a group of close friends in the area. And, of course, she bred and sold dogs in her spare time. Not bad. Hard work, of course, but Judy clearly is not one to mind that while she is handling horses. She seems to have a very large horse gene.

When I asked Judy whether a love of horses was in her family background, she told me that her grandfather was a blacksmith who kept two horses and a buggy at his shop and that her uncle had a two-hundred-acre farm with a bull, milking cows, chickens, pigs, and a separate horse barn. Particularly fascinating to Judy is that this uncle rode on the same trails in the 1940s and 1950s where she herself has ridden for the past twenty-plus years. The continuance of the horse gene seems quite clear.

That gene has remained in the family, not only with Judy but with several daughters and granddaughters as well. Judy herself first began riding at summer camps in her early teen years. When in high school, she and her best friend would save babysitting money to rent horses on Sunday afternoons. Then came marriage and children. In 1969, Judy's eight-year-old daughter asked if she could learn to ride. At this time the family lived in a farmhouse on a twelve-acre piece of country land that also had a carriage barn. This was the beginning of horse ownership for Judy and her family. First they acquired an older, quiet horse as a teacher, and then two years later a handsome six-year-old Morgan gelding, who became the daughter's equitation horse. Then came a three-year-old Quarter Horse for Judy herself. After her youngest daughter learned to ride, they spent many enjoyable hours together on nearby trails and at horse shows on Sundays. She and her husband often trailered across town to a beautiful conservation area to ride.

Shortly after Judy's family began riding, horse people in the area started a club called North County Riding and Driving Club, which grew by leaps and bounds. Established for families, the club held meetings every month to educate the members and to plan horse shows. For more than twenty years, there were also breakfast trail rides in nearby state forests and pot luck suppers. Judy was an officer of the club and an active member. Finally, in the nineties, with women holding down jobs and television gaining in popularity, the club disbanded.

Life changed when Judy's children went off to college. She and her husband purchased a twenty-five-acre farm in a nearby town, and her dream of a running a riding school began to come true. She already had a master's degree and several years of teaching, so she felt prepared to teach, applying the same principles in her riding school that she had successfully used in teaching English. In the summer of 1975, she and her husband built an outdoor ring, fenced seven pastures, and refurbished the barn. Judy commented, "This was hard work!" And I am sure it was. In 1978, they added an indoor arena and ten stalls.

The late 1970s, when Judy was in her mid forties, were an exciting time for her. The riding school had many facets. The regular schedule included children's lessons during the week at 4 PM and on Saturdays with adult classes in the evenings. Horses were turned out every morning to rest, as well as all day Wednesday and Sunday. Judy also had contracts for physical education credits with students from the nearby college and with a private high school for ten-week sessions. Then for two summers, exchange students came for a six-week course. The first year, there were seven boys from Italy, Spain, and Japan, all of whom spoke perfect English and planned to attend U.S. colleges. The second year, one girl and six boys from Iraq came, with the girl translating for the boys. Both groups were attentive and interested, so they progressed rapidly.

Not only did she start a riding school, but in 1976 Judy became a local horse club and 4-H leader with monthly meetings at her home. Parents helped carpool children to hay rides, polo games, equine demonstrations, and such. There was a horse show every year that raised money to send the children to a week of horse camp in Spencer. It was in 1975 that Judy bought Princess, a lovely 15.3-hand Morgan mare not only to use in the school but also to breed. Princess had her first foal in 1977, a filly that Judy kept and which became the grandmother of Gracie, Judy's last and much-loved horse.

In 1980, Judy started a summer riding camp for day students from 8:30 AM to 4:30 PM with a lesson each morning and

151

afternoon. She hired as helpers college girls and boys who both enjoyed children and were experienced riders. A few years later, she established a drill team of accomplished girl riders who put on demonstrations for a yearly open house and at some schooling shows. The list of Judy's work with children also included taking four or five students to local 4-H shows each summer, where they learned how to prepare horses for showing and the techniques of the sport. Parents again were very supportive, providing lunch and enthusiasm.

*Judy at 73 with her horse Gracie after riding with friends in Rutland State Forest*

Another major change occurred in 1986. After more than ten years of teaching riding and running riding schools, when their children were grown, some married, and grandchildren arriving, Judy and her husband decided to sell the farm and move to their present home. Here on more than five acres of land, they built a four-stall barn with tack room and supply room, with a cleared pasture and more land available for clearing. They brought along a dressage horse, a trail horse, and Gracie, the Trakehner-Morgan bred by Judy and the granddaughter of Princess. Training began with Gracie at three years of age, but only at four did Judy feel the mare was ready to be trained to saddle. Then began many years of pleasure rides with neighboring friends. She sold her other horses and took in two boarders, one owned by a former student and the other by a close friend, who shared responsibility with her for the barn work. They remained with her almost thirteen years. In 2000, Judy became interested in twenty-five-mile competitive rides so began conditioning Gracie and for several years enjoyed participating in those.

Life changed again a year or so ago. Her boarders' owners, whose lives also were in flux, removed their horses from her farm, which meant that Judy by herself would have to do all the work for her horse that the boarders had previously shared as part of their board payment. And then, to top it all, came the ice storm of December 2008. For a full week, there was no water, no electricity, no heat, and still a horse to care for. It was the final straw. Judy made the hard decision. Her Gracie, now twenty-three years old, would have to leave. Fortunately, Judy was able to place her at the home of a friend, where she would be well cared for, loved, and enjoyed.

I had wondered when I first arrived at this well-set-up horse farm why there was nary a horse on the property. "Why no horses now?" boldly said I. Judy quickly explained that the last winter was an especially hard one, and the work to maintain the single horse she had by then was just too much. It was time for her to stop feeding and caring for horses. Now, I cared for three horses myself last year in two barns on either side of my property, and I am three years older than she. And she is in much better physical condition than I. Judy has no problems with shoulders, knees, hips, back. She is a relatively small woman, but with the stable work she has done in past years, you know she must be physically stronger than she looks. In other words, I still wondered.

So I started to probe a bit, suggesting that perhaps she, like me, found she tired more easily than usual. Her response was equivocal, as she said that yes, by the end of the day, she supposed she is somewhat tired. Perhaps, I suggested, she is finding herself less confident as she aged, noting that a gradual loss of confidence in everyday activities is common to people in their seventies. I got a response that left me in no doubt that she is fully as confident with horses as she ever was.

Only on writing this piece has it occurred to me that maybe she is an example of the "been there, done that" syndrome that sometimes occurs in late middle age. Judy was moving from work with horses to just play with horses. She had taught riding, bred nine foals, trained numerous horses, run various riding schools, and done stable work for many years. Then she had dropped the teaching, breeding, and much of the training, but retained the stable work, riding more just for pleasure with others. And finally she has dropped the stable work also, leaving open the possibility of riding just for pleasure. She had moved from a horse career with heavy and steady work to a situation in which horses would be just for pleasure. This is what many of us start and end with, namely, riding for fun. This is one more step in her gradual retirement from her life's major occupation.

Judy had begun by simply saying that she had got rid of all her horses and virtually stopped riding because of family constraints. Later, she explained more fully. She and her husband Bob have done a fair amount of traveling and still have many places on their list that they want to visit. But how can they travel when they have a horse and no boarders to care for her? As we talked about all Judy's horse years, she suggested that perhaps in earlier years she had spent too much time doing the horse thing.

It was just this past spring of 2009 that Gracie left her home with Judy. This is the mare who is the granddaughter of the first horse she bred. Seeing Gracie leave must have been very hard. I asked if she missed her horses and received an emphatic "yes, terribly." I am personally not convinced that Judy will never own another horse or that she will not ride whatever horse her friends make available to her. In fact, lately she admitted to vaguely thinking about leasing a horse for a summer only. She is a healthy seventy-seven. That horse gene of hers is a big one indeed. I am betting on that gene to find some way to get her back in the saddle.

*Beth Jenkins at 58 on Geronimo*

# BETH JENKINS

## Age 70
## Sherborn

I admit that my interview with Beth Jenkins surprised me, experienced as I am at speaking with horse people about their activities. My interview with Beth happened to be my thirty-second interview with a horse person and the sixteenth for this book of twenty. I have developed a pattern of starting with a few standard questions and then letting it roll as it will from there. Trying to be more or less chronological, I usually ask when the person began riding. Beth responded in a vague manner, saying she supposed at the age of seven or eight, when her older sister bought a horse. Next I asked if as a young girl she was horse crazy, fully expecting her to say "yes" and begin to elaborate. Instead, Beth thought for a minute and then said that she really didn't know if that was so. With women, the answer I expect and almost always receive is an emphatic "yes."

Realizing that here I had someone different, I jumped to questions I usually ask toward the end of interviews for this book. Did she still ride, and if she had stopped, how did she handle it? "Oh," she responded. "I guess I haven't ridden for about ten years when my last horse died. But anytime I wanted I could ride one of my four boarders' horses. I just haven't wanted to." Now, Beth has been a dressage rider, instructor, and judge and extremely active for years in the New England Dressage Association (NEDA). Whoa, thought I. This will be different and fascinating.

It seems that her mother was closer to being horse crazy than Beth. They lived in Chicago near what is now O'Hare airport and which at that time was a huge cattle ranch. Her mother used to go over to a nearby stable and ride other people's horses for them midweek. This stable was a very ordinary one with about fifteen horses, most owned apparently by women. Beth

157

supposed they were single women working in Chicago who liked to ride on weekends in the nearby Forest Preserves. Her mother would ride a five-gaited show horse, and Beth would be put on some quiet horse—which took care of Beth while her mother enjoyed her riding.

When Beth was about thirteen years old, the family left the Chicago area for Barrington, Illinois, twenty miles further out of the city. For about five years, she and her cousin, Susie Sexton (who went on to become a prominent equestrian photgrapher until her death last year), apparently had a ball riding and exercising other people's horses. They did this a lot, "begging and borrowing whatever horse we could," and because they were then in hunt country, many horses and trails were available. They just rode "by the seat of our pants," not thinking of riding lessons, for there were no funds available anyway.

Beth graduated from the University of Pennsylvania in 1961, married in 1962, and put her husband through Wharton business school in Philadelphia. At first they lived in Walpole, and Beth decided she wanted a horse. As she tells the story, her husband's enthusiasm for this project was expressed by the offer of five hundred dollars to cover the horse and horse expenses forever. She managed to find Yankee, a 16-hand gray mix of a horse, for only three hundred dollars, because he had a healed quarter crack on one hoof that kept splitting. Her vet said that if she kept a radiator clamp around the hoof she could ride him, which she did for fifteen years. There was barely two hundred of the five hundred dollars left, so Beth advertised in the *Boston Globe* that she had two stalls for rent, and before long a nurse by the name of Helen brought Dolly to her stable. Dolly stayed for many years. Beth did a lot of work on the property, while she and Helen "had horses and rode."

In 1968, Beth and her husband, Frank, bought their present house in Sherborn, complete with a metal shop that was just waiting in Beth's imagination to become a horse barn. She had also set herself up as a computer software specialist, working part-time for Honeywell, so she had a bit more cash. The night before the move from Walpole to Sherborn, she and Helen rode their horses down the road to Sherborn, a journey of about twelve miles. No trailer. When the move took place next day, lo and behold, there were two horses loose, wandering around the improperly fenced property. Not long after, Beth and her husband, by hand, dug fifty-six post holes to make a reliable fence for horses.

The move to Sherborn provided Beth with about seventy-five miles of trails. Most of the surrounding woods are in conservation or town forest and connect to the Dover trails. Because the area is built on a ledge and glacial hardpan, there are no town sewer and water, so houses are and must remain far apart. The area cries out for horses, and there are a lot of them there. Beth improved her barn and fencing and added boarders. Meanwhile, she and her husband have turned a very simple house into a beautiful and modern one.

In 1969, Beth decided, after riding safely for about twenty years untutored, that she would take riding lessons. This occurred after she competed on her horse Yankee in a show at Sunshine Farm near Framingham. She was riding against sophisticated people with long years of horse knowledge behind them, and she came away in last place with nary a ribbon. This would not do.

Soon Beth became acquainted with people connected with the larger equestrian world and specifically with the developing dressage group. In Sherborn, there was Meg Plum, an official for the Federation Equestrian Internationale (FEI) in Switzerland. Meg recommended Beth to Pamela Fitzwilliam, a dressage trainer, who lived twenty-five miles away and who worked for Priscilla Endicott, founder of the fledgling New England

Dressage Associaton (NEDA). Beth realized that she needed a horse trailer if she was going to participate with this dressage group. Although her finances were looking up at this point, she did not waste much money on the trailer, acquiring a green plywood, one-horse trailer built on a Model A Ford axle. Beth laughed, "It looked like an outhouse."

At this point, Beth bought for $250 a trotting Standardbred gelding straight off the track, named Comet, and with great effort taught him to canter. She expected that Pamela Fitzwilliam would advise her to replace this horse, but instead Pamela declared, "This is a great horse!" And so began Beth's dressage work, with lessons, which over the next several years included instruction with Karl Mikolka, Bill Woods, and Sally Swift.

I noted that the switch from the carefree ride-as-you-can approach of her youth to dressage in her maturity was a very big one. Beth said that she liked the precision of dressage, that it "zeroed in on my psyche." She started competing and getting more training. She worked for several years with Anders Lindgren from Sweden, who specialized in teaching instructors to teach. A by-product of this experience was a new interest in body awareness, with influence from Sally Swift and the Alexander Technique. Soon she constructed a flat area on her property suitable for dressage practice. Beth started teaching lessons herself and running clinics, and soon many riders were coming in and out. In 1977 she acquired her judging license and judged actively for eighteen years. She had developed a good eye for the body movements of horse and rider and found as much or more pleasure off the horse as on. She particularly enjoyed teaching and says that she is "a better teacher than rider."

Meanwhile, Beth had replaced Comet with a homebred part Thoroughbred named Lukhi and then a full Thoroughbred, Bay Native. Over the years, each of these "retired" to carrying her children around the Sherborn trails. By the mid-eighties, the

European warmblood horses were "the thing" in the dressage world, and Beth bought an Oldenburg, Geronimo, who turned out to be her last horse. He died in 1998. Beth by that time was heavily into NEDA work and did not replace him—and so ended her riding days, almost by chance.

NEDA was just starting in the 1970s, and Beth had got in on the ground floor. Her computer and organizational skills made her valuable, and as the group grew, she handled membership, website development, sponsorship, and financial processes. She worked with show management for more than thirty years. She joined the NEDA board in 1972 and soon started the NEDA Summer "Whatucanner" Show, for those doing "What-U-Can" on their horses. She conducted "Riding Through Winter" seminars from 1987 until 1991, a five-week unmounted program on dressage basics and body awareness.

In 1990 she took over the NEDA Fall Festival as secretary, moving to manager in 1996. This festival is a very big deal for dressage riders. It consists of a five-day competition that is probably the largest dressage show in the United States. Except for the show office staff, it is run completely by volunteers. Almost six hundred horses compete in about fourteen hundred rides in six rings. Beth received recognition for her service to dressage when the U.S. Dressage Federation named her its national volunteer of the year in 2009 for consistent volunteer work in the dressage world. Beth remains at the heart of NEDA.

And why has hale and hearty Beth, at a mere seventy years of age, not been riding horseback at all and completely pulled back from her teaching and judging? She says she has a full life as is with her family, tennis three times a week, and various other activities she enjoys, including of course NEDA involvement. She does not miss either riding or horse care. I mentioned in an earlier sketch that about the age of sixty there often comes a desire for change. We realize that we have possibly another twenty years of active life before us, and we say to some of the activities we have previously enjoyed, "Been there, done that. On to something else." I suspect that Beth may feel that way about riding.

Meanwhile, Beth has four horse boarders (who run the barn as a co-op), three horses and one pony to admire, and, as she says, the only work she does for the boarders is depositing the monthly checks. That and her close involvement with the dressage scene seems currently to satisfy her passion for horses.

*Sy Cote at 72 "taking the cow down the fence," demonstrating control of the cow in the cattle segment of the Working Ranch Horse Class at an Eastern Mountain Ranch Horse Association show in New York in 2008*

# SY COTE

## Age 74
## Granby

For Sy and his horse Ranch Hand Peppy, playing with cows is the name of the game. Behind the Cote home on their twenty-nine-acre property is a 120- by 240-foot arena with cow pen, ready for action. When the grass grows to the proper height, the neighbor's cows will be released onto the pasture for summer grazing and occasional fun for Sy and Peppy, a shiny black nine-year-old Quarter Horse gelding waiting nearby in an eight-stall barn. He has the company of a twenty-seven-year-old buckskin Quarter Horse gelding, IMA Sly Skipper, used now only for occasional trail riding, no longer for cowboy games. Sy grooms and rides Peppy for an hour or two daily.

It all started sixty-five years ago in Chicopee when nine-year-old Sy wandered into a riding stable and became instantly fascinated with horses. His learning about horses began right then as a stable boy, cleaning up and doing all the lowly jobs required. Sy says, with justifiable pride, that everything he knows about riding and horses was gained from hands-on-experience, not lessons and school courses. He learned "by the seat of my pants." As a teenager, he rode for horse owners at a private stable and particularly enjoyed gymkhana activities. He remembers that he bought his first horse, a grade mare named Chiquita, from Louis Goodyear in Sunderland. Then came Peanuts, a grade Quarter Horse gelding, and it was with him that Sy, at the age of seventeen, began showing in stock horse classes. That marked the start of a long career of showing, both his own and other people's horses, in Western competitions.

Then there was the Bar Ten Riding Club, consisting of ten young men, all Western riding enthusiasts, who leased a Granby barn for their horses. During this time, Sy was also riding sales horses in Canaan, Connecticut. Then at age twenty-one came Sy's life-changing Texas experience. A local contractor bought

165

four cutting horse mares from Texas and brought them east along with the services of an authentic cowboy. A turnback was needed for the sport, and so Sy played that part and began to get the fever. He went off to Texas in the fall of 1957 with the cowboy and took a cattle ranch job for several months, working with 750 head of first-calf heifers, who require careful work by the mounted cowboys. Sy's learning progressed, and he bought himself a cutting horse stallion for the then astronomical sum of

*Sy with his horse Ranch Hand Peppy dragging a log in a trail horse competition at Cazenovia College in New York in 2005*

two thousand dollars. He worked with the horse, showing him in primarily Western pleasure trail classes, sometimes reining, and won numerous year-end awards in the New England Horse Council, the Massachusetts Horse Council, and the Connecticut Horse Show Association.

Since high school years, Sy had been working in construction with heavy equipment. He continued to do so for forty-three years, until retiring at age sixty-three. In 1960, at the age of twenty-four, he married Judy, and off they went back to Texas

166

on their honeymoon, where Sy bought Judy a young filly who eventually was bred and produced a half dozen foals. This led to the beginning of a training career, because the man who bought the filly's first foal, Rim Rock Joe, needed the horse trained and thought Sy was the man to do it.

In 1964, Sy and Judy bought their present property in Granby and eventually produced and raised three children. Their two sons learned to ride horses but quickly found motorcycles more to their liking. Their daughter, however, became a horse woman and now lives on the far edge of the Cote property, helping out with Sy's horses as necessary. Early on with a friend's help, Sy built their present barn close behind their house.

From the early sixties to the mid-eighties, Sy became active in Quarter Horse shows. He is a charter member of the New England Quarter Horse Association (NEQHA), serving on its board of directors. He also became a part-time trainer and was often asked by other horse people to show their horses, particularly in halter classes. He helped his daughter ride and show during this period and was very active in Western Quarter Horse shows at a time when Western showing was growing in popularity.

In 1984 he spent one hectic year breeding a stallion for a friend from Maine. He built what he calls a "mare motel" with eight stalls and bred eighteen mares with the stallion, getting advice and help from a local veterinarian and using artificial insemination. Sy says that one year of that, in addition to his regular construction job, was more than enough.

Then abruptly, in 1985, he took a year off from showing and training and instead worked on expanding his and Judy's home, confining his equine activities to trail riding. He had also been increasingly concerned about some of the new methods being used to train Quarter Horses so that he felt

167

a time-out was a good idea. Practices and fashions change in the horse world as they do in other areas, and one of these changes was taking place in the Quarter Horse field. Massachusetts riders, particularly in the eastern section of the state, had been largely riding English, favoring such horses as the Thoroughbred and particularly the Morgan. Gradually, Western riding was catching on, especially in the western part of the state, and that meant more Quarter Horses and more Western showing, and the start of the NEQHA.

By the late eighties and early nineties, another and more positive change was taking place in Western riding that caught Sy's eye and mind. This was the Versatility movement, emphasizing development of the Quarter Horse in a "natural" way, as a horse bred and trained for work on Western ranches. At Heritage Farm in nearby Northampton, the Rauschers were onto the new movement, organizing competitions in practical activities such as team penning. Sy rode, competed, and judged shows at Heritage Farm for about eight years.

Because I know little about competitions in Western-style riding, I asked Sy to explain what is meant by Versatility competitions. He noted first of all—and this says a lot—that no silver is allowed on the saddles of the riders. Business, not glitter, is the order of the day. There are five classes: ranch horse riding (basically a pleasure class), ranch trail, ranch cutting, working ranch horse (as in reining patterns and boxing of cattle and fencing, then roping), and conformation. Sy believes that horses actively enjoy these activities with cattle, because there is variety, challenge, and the fun of dominating another animal. I think he speaks for himself as well as his horse in this statement. He thinks that working with cattle is "the best thing you can do for a horse, because it has his interest." Although Sy has an amateur card, he still competes in open divisions against professional trainers.

Then in 2004, another horse entered Sy's life. His daughter telephoned him and said she had found the perfect horse for him in Galleton, Tennessee, a three-year-old green-broke Quarter Horse gelding. After careful consideration, he bought the horse, convinced by his conformation, breeding, and exceptionally agreeable disposition. At first he hesitated, feeling the horse was perhaps not sufficiently responsive, but over time and with training, the gelding has developed sufficient responsiveness. This is the black Quarter Horse still in Sy's stable—Ranch Hand Peppy, a horse he shows once or twice a month in three seasons.

Peppy has become a winner for his master. In recent years, he won the high point all-around versatility ranch horse award at numerous shows. Sy has taken him to the Equine Affaire in Springfield, where in 2007 the Versatility Challenge Competition was added. This competition accepts only thirty-two horses on the basis of videos submitted. In 2007 Sy and Peppy won fourth; in 2008 Sy was ill and did not compete; and in 2009 they won fifth.

Since retirement, Sy and Judy have left for warmer climes in the winters, for eight years to Arizona and for the last few years to Florida, taking Peppy with them, of course, for casual trail riding. When asked whether he was thinking of quitting riding, since he has had several serious illnesses in the last few years, Sy—not unexpectedly—responded that he would "never quit riding—only when they put me in the ground." Asked for any changes to accommodate his increasing age, he responded that he really hasn't made any. He still wears no riding helmet, although obviously he must have worn a hard hat doing construction work. Not tall, but agile and trim, he can still mount from the ground. And he continues to ride alone, although he often enjoys the company of a neighboring horseman.

It is obvious that Sy isn't thinking about aging and no longer riding. He has his mind on that arena and cow pen out back and is watching his grass grow taller for the neighbor's cows.

*Pat Kane at 69 with Candy*

# PAT KANE
## 69
### Belchertown

"Game" is probably the summary word to describe Pat Kane. She is the youngest of those interviewed for this book (sixty-nine at the time we spoke) and also the person who started to follow her passion for horses at the latest age (fifty-nine). During those ten years, between the beginning and the present, however, she has done a heck of a lot of riding and learning.

Pat was brought up near Hamden Pond not far from Westfield with few opportunities to get astride even a pony. From the ages of eighteen to twenty-six, she managed to ride a few times at dude ranches. For a few years, she was happily escorting her younger daughter to riding lessons and horse shows.

Meanwhile, she and her husband had bought a three-and-a-half-acre property with a garage turned into a barn behind it. She finally fulfilled her lifelong dream of owning a horse when she discovered Red and rescued him from a bad situation. She says that he was by no means her dream horse, skinny and standing in manure up to his knees. Furthermore, she soon found that he was very skillful at getting loose, having done so at his former home in order to find something to eat. Pat brought him home, fed him regularly, and lavished him with attention. He blossomed into a handsome gelding, "as sweet and gentle as they come." Although completely unskilled, she rode him as often as she could, having only learned a few basics on paid trail rides.

Pat tells a remarkable story about the pony Ginger, who replaced Red. She had been purchased from a family in Belchertown who had owned her for several years. Previously, however, the pony had been with a family who lived about twenty miles away and whose riding daughter was going away to college. After being some months with the Kane family, somehow the pony got loose and traveled all twenty miles

173

back to her original home. Although Pat knew that she and her daughters had taken good care of Ginger, appearances were otherwise, and she says she felt mortified. Two trail horses followed, Bucky and Roper, mainly for her daughters, but they had to be sold as expenses for the children grew.

Life went on, and Pat was fully occupied by her bookkeeping job at the University of Massachusetts, Amherst, where both daughters graduated and where she worked for twenty-seven years. She was (and is) an enthusiastic gardener, so her job and her garden left her little time for anything else. Horses, however, remained on her mind. Finally, at the age of fifty-nine, she began elementary riding lessons at a nearby stable, where she discovered and bought Sonny, a very mild and slow sort of horse.

Feeling ready for a faster and more challenging horse, she soon acquired Paco, a Paso Fino gelding who left her with a broken arm the first time she mounted him. When she had tried him out, he was fine in the ring and on the road. However, once she put down her money and brought him to the stable, she discovered she had a very different and difficult horse. It was two-and-a-half years ago that a fall off this horse led to a badly broken arm and the immediate departure of Paco plus, of course, a period of no riding and a loss of confidence. She eventually gave him away to someone who specialized in the breed and enjoyed horses with lots of brio.

Pat's next horse was Candy, a Rocky Mountain gaited mare with a sweet disposition but a growing tendency to spook and bolt. When her younger daughter, Kerri, built a house and barn not far off and bought a horse, Pat moved her horse there and rode a bit with her daughter.

It wasn't until Kerri sold her house that Pat's riding life really took off. She moved Candy to a different stable in Belchertown, run by a cowboy sort of man who enjoys taking his boarders on riding excursions all over the area. Pat, a very friendly and outgoing person, loved these trips and the camaraderie. She also met Chris, who is happy to have Pat ride with her on one of her four horses, two of which are draft horses.

At present, Pat is living in a beautiful condominium just a few miles north of the center of Belchertown. She moved there in September 2007, about two-and-a-half years after her husband died. She has been working about two days a week at UMass and plans soon to give up her job completely. Then she must make a difficult choice. If she wants to handle the expense of boarding a horse, she must move to less expensive housing, giving up the comfortable home that she just moved into two years ago.

Pat has already made one very difficult decision to sell or otherwise arrange for the departure of Candy, because she no longer feels safe on her. Candy has dumped her—or caused a quick dismount—multiple times while shying, spinning, and bolting. The mare also tries to bite or kick her as she dismounts. Pat has discovered that her present saddles do not fit the mare properly, possibly causing the horse pain, but the problem is deeper, because now she has lost confidence in the horse. Until Pat can find the mare a new home, she will continue to pay board at her present stable. That decision made, if she is to ride—and I suspect that decision has already been made— she must find an appropriate horse and affordable house, downsizing her home for the second time in only a few years.

If this situation sounds depressing, I must say that Pat doesn't find it so. She is an upbeat woman with a faith that accepts what happens and expects a bright and exciting future. She says she does the hard work of exploring possibilities and fact-finding and then thinks things will fall into place eventually.

Until she acquires a new horse and new home, Pat will not be without opportunities to ride. She and her daughter plan a four-week trip for the Red Rock Ride out West. They will go to

Las Vegas, and then the riding guests will be trucked around to ride at places like Bryce Canyon and Zion National Park. Pat thoroughly enjoyed it three times before and expects to enjoy it equally another time.

Back home, while waiting to find a home for Candy and to discover the right horse to buy, she has the opportunity of riding with her friend Chris and also riding horses down at the Blue Star Equiculture horse sanctuary and organic farm in Palmer. This is a charity that Pat has embraced. Its mission is "to provide retired working horses a sanctuary and homeless working horses the opportunity to be useful and positively improve their lives, while bringing education, equine awareness, skills and healing to the community and the environment." She expects to work there as a volunteer, helping to care for the horses. As for mucking stalls, undoubtedly a major task offered, she said emphatically, "I love to muck," declaring how wonderful all the smells are. I am not sure we would all agree. She also hopes to help with the gardening at the sanctuary.

Pat is an active member of the Granby Regional Horse Council (GRHC), where she is a board member and treasurer of its Belchertown chapter. The horse sanctuary and the GRHC will both keep her in contact with horses and horse people even when she becomes unable to ride—which she cannot now envision. She enthusiastically declares, "I want to ride until they have to pry me out of the saddle." Her one wish is to "find a horse that will take me into my eighties." She looks forward to a horse-filled future, beginning with more riding lessons to help her regain her confidence. As for the horse she plans to buy, she has compiled a list of ten qualities to look for, saying that eight out of ten will do. As the owner of her present stable has told her, "You can't ride pretty."

I think Pat's approach has to do with a new maturity as she nears her seventies. She feels that "quality of life has become more important." She wants to take more care of her body and is attempting to eat like a vegan to improve her health. There is a new sense of limited time and an increasing appreciation of what life can offer in the area where she derives most pleasure. And she is going for it. After all, she will only be seventy years old on her next birthday.

*Polly Bartlett at 81 with her Norwegian Fjord, Civian,*
*taking a break after riding to the top of the ski area at*
*Eaglebrook School in Deerfield*

# POLLY BARTLETT

## Age 82
## Shelburne Falls

It all started in Vermont. When Polly at the age of eight went off to Camp Kenjocketee, she fell head over heels in love with her riding instructor—none other than a young Sally Swift. Returning to the camp, the horses, and Sally became the highlight of Polly's life for the next seven years. Her admiration of the well-known Sally Swift did not diminish when she became an adult. She named her first daughter Sally after her idol, and about fifteen years ago took her daughter and granddaughter to a clinic run by Sally Swift.

Polly's auspicious start with horses continued with her determination to make horses her life's work, not an easy task in the 1940s. During her final three years of high school, she worked at Endsmeet Farm, a "gentleman's" farm, where she acquired some practical experience with using horses for work. While there, she had a harrowing experience when she had the job of attaching a horse to a dump rake and driving him out to collect the hay left on the ground. When she started on the edge of the field, the rake caught in the fence, and in the melee that followed, she barely avoided being wounded in the neck by the wheel—which was almost, but not quite, the end of Polly.

Not to be deterred, she took a pre-veterinarian course at Penn State, switching to animal husbandry. She rode and taught there, and finally acquired her own horse, Wake Robin, a four- or five-year-old Cleveland Bay, who dumped her in her senior year, breaking her back. Still aiming for a life with horses, she worked on a breeding farm, taking over the nighttime watch for mares to foal. Next came Washington State for graduate work, an interesting experience but with very little riding.

Finally, Polly returned to the University of Massachusetts at Amherst, and here she had the opportunity to ride the well-

179

known Morgan stallion Panez in a Morgan show. She showed me a picture of herself on Panez. She also met and married her present husband, David. As often happens during early marriage and child-bearing years, riding was postponed until it was time for her children to begin with horses. Skiing became the family sport. Polly was on the ski patrol at the Berkshire East slopes for thirty-four years, finally deciding that she wanted no more icy moguls and increasingly difficult qualifying tests. Now she skis with friends and also does cross-country skiing.

Other occupations over the years have been as a half-time physical education teacher for primary grades for three years, picking and preserving a large vegetable garden, making her own bread and granola, and sewing clothing. She also serves on various conservation committees, including the group that presents the Riverfest on the Deerfield River. Add to that her present work in the Shelburne Falls Trolley Museum, actually operating the hand pump car herself to the delight of visitors. Since she encourages her customers to help with the job, she calls it an "opportunity for a cooperative experience." Obviously, Polly's life has been full even without horses.

But back to horses. In 1974, she acquired a half-Arabian sorrel gelding named Eric the Red, and the next year came a green Morgan gelding named Toddy. Both horses needed training, which Polly gradually gave them to the best of her ability, considering time constraints while managing a home and family. Eric the Red continued to show the less reliable traits of many Arabians, while Toddy eventually became that wonderful horse that "anyone can ride." During the next twenty-five years, Polly ran a 4-H club, riding all over the hills in Shelburne Falls and neighboring Buckland.

The location of the Bartletts' home is relevant to all that happened next with her horses, both good and bad. They live right along Route 112, just one mile from the intersection with Route 2. Trails abound, but so do roads—well-traveled roads. For some years, Polly's two horses had grazing rights in an orchard across Route 112, and Polly used to take them over there in the evening and return them to their home area at night. She thoroughly enjoyed doing this evening ritual. By oneself, however, this is a tricky maneuver. And Polly did it bareback. At one point on the return, Eric the Red decided to attack Toddy, while Polly was riding him. In the ensuing mayhem, Eric's powerful kick hit Polly's lower leg, breaking it, but she was still astride Toddy. Luckily, girls on the local cross country running team were coming down the road. Two of the girls knew Polly and her horses and came to her rescue, box-splinting her leg by the time her husband came home. Despite such incidents, Eric the Red and Toddy were used yearly in the local fourth of July parades and remained with Polly until their deaths at the ages of twenty-four and twenty-five years old.

Horseless, Polly tried leases and loans of various horses. She missed taking caring of them as much as riding them. Meanwhile, she was riding with her daughter, who lives nearby and owns several horses. But that was not enough. Then in 2001 a registered Norwegian Fjord mare, Civian, became available, supposedly bombproof. This nineteen-year-old mare already had given birth to ten foals, but she seemed in good health. The problem with Civian has been her urge to be part of a herd, and when ridden with other horses, to be the leader. Polly thinks she is very lonely. Civian's natural pace is not fast enough to remain ahead of the other horses in a group ride, so the mare either pulls or jigs. She has not been a pleasure to ride under those circumstances. She does cross water well, which is odd, because when she first came to Polly's barn, she would not even go near the brook. Now she does it only in summer. All horses have their idiosyncrasies.

Not to be deterred, Polly with her daughter's help took Civian to the New England Fjord show in Woodstock, Vermont, in 2003, where she entered her in pleasure, equitation, and trail classes. She says that they did not perform up to Civian's ability. Her daughter took videos of her riding Civian, and Polly judged herself harshly.

Polly has twice gone off Civian, the first time on her initial ride when the accompanying horse left for home and Civian wanted to go home with him. The second time happened just this past October, 2009. This was scary. It was a beautiful fall day, and after hand grazing Civian, Polly saddled her up and rode her in the home pasture at a walk. All was going well, and both horse and rider seemed happy and relaxed, so Polly decided to cross the road and go up the hill for the fine pasture to be had there. So up they went to the top, when all of a sudden a big, brown bale of hay appeared unannounced. Civian swung round in one of her 180s, bolted, and started to run pell mell downhill toward her home—and of course the road. Polly tried to circle her to no avail and was thrown off, landing on her hip but amazingly not breaking any bones. Fortunately, neighbors saw her on the hill and realized what was happening. They quickly stopped cars on Route 112, and someone went up the hill to help Polly. The experience brought home again to Polly two truths. Horses are unpredictable, and at eighty-two she is not as strong as she used to be.

Polly seems very relaxed and accepting of her past, present, and future with horses, which seems to have been her approach to the various difficult horses she has owned and gradually trained. Now she is aware that her legs and arms are becoming less strong and that this weakness, along with various other physical problems, keeps her from riding with safety and pleasure in the ways she had previously. Trotting and cantering are no longer feasible, but she does enjoy walking on Civian. Her daughter sensibly prefers that her mother only ride with her. Because Polly "enjoys chores and saving apple and carrot scraps for her," Civian seems assured of a lifetime in her pasture. And Polly seems equally confident of more pleasure with her old mare.

*Lyn Howard at 71 driving her Morgans, Galen and Max, at the GMHA competition in South Woodstock, Vermont*

# LYN HOWARD

## Age 72
## Richmond

At seventy-two, Lyn Howard is pressing onward and upward. Apparently she has not heard the general opinion that, on reaching seventy years of age, one should slow down, pull back a bit, and certainly not forge ahead into new territory. Because that is what she is doing, expanding her abilities in the difficult and sometimes dangerous equine specialty of carriage driving competition. An energetic person, she welcomes the challenge.

Lyn admits with a smile that she began competing early, at the age of four, in East Anglia, Great Britain, when she won what was called a horse brass at the local pony club in a walk and trot class. Her family lived on a farm. In England during World War II, no gasoline was available, so all farmers worked their land with draft horses. The easygoing chestnut Suffolk Punch was especially popular in East Anglia. Growing up, Lyn learned to turn over the hay with a horse rake, to start and stop the cart as hay was forked, and then drive the load back for stacking. Before and after the harvest season, all horses were newly shod, and it was Lyn's job to ride them over to the "smythie" about four miles away. As a teenager, she also helped the next door farmer break his young horse stock. He had been an Australian cowboy, moving cattle and fixing fences. He broke his horses quietly, not rodeo style, and he needed someone light on their back while he longed them. That someone was usually Lyn.

Lyn is a physician, educated and trained at Oxford University. As a fourth-year student she visited the U.S. for three months, working first at Cornell Medical College in New York City and then at Kansas University Medical Center. After returning to England to graduate and do an internship, she came back to the States to marry a Kansas man and complete an internal medicine residency at the University of Colorado. Her

185

first child was born during those years. She continued to ride with friends who had a ranch just outside Kansas City, and in fact she remembers actually nursing her six-week-old child while on horseback. For her second child she went back to the family farm in England, where a midwife helped her deliver the baby.

Lyn returned to the United States for a fellowship at Vanderbilt and then joined the faculty at the Albany Medical Center in 1972. She slowly climbed the academic ladder of medicine and reached the status of full professor in 1988, retiring after thirty-six years in practice. Her specialty is clinical nutrition, difficult research-based work not to be confused with general dietetics. She wrote more than eighty research papers and chapters for major medical textbooks and has felt great dedication to her research and the people whose lives she was following closely. So much for Lyn's professional life.

Peace issues have always been important to Lyn. She is a Quaker, and in her early twenties in London she joined a nonviolent U.S. group walking from San Francisco to Moscow. She spent a few days in jail along the way, as often happened to idealistic groups of young people in the early sixties. Since that time, she has done considerable foreign travel. One example of particular interest to horse people is a month-long excursion in 2005 to Mongolia, where she and her husband rode the native horses on a camping expedition in the Gobi desert and over the wide open steppes. She showed me a scrapbook of pictures of that trip, including many scenes she herself had sketched along the way.

Lyn has been living on a 110-acre farm in Poestenkill, New York, just across the Massachusetts border. She introduced her children to horses early, at one time having sixteen ponies on the property, mostly the Welsh variety. Her children participated in 4-H and later in Pony Club. She and her twelve-year-old daughter began eventing in 1980 when Lyn was in her early forties (a wonderful time of life for riding).

Six horses now make their home with Lyn. There are two Morgans for pair driving (Max and Galen), a twenty-four-year-old Morgan that has been driving "forever," a Quarter Horse for general riding, and two minis for the pleasure of her grandchildren, of whom she has nine. She attends from ten to twelve competitive carriage events (both pleasure and combined driving) a year, including sleigh rallies. On her farm she has a

*Lyn at 67 with Farthing, her 36-inch minihorse*
full-size outdoor driving arena and about two miles of drivable trails, which she uses four times a week. She also trailers her horses to state parks and various dirt road areas for recreational drives. The same energy that fueled her in her medical profession has been turned toward driving, with the ultimate aim of mastering the complicated sport of pair driving.

For help with her driving horses, she has sensibly turned for instruction to a professional trainer in Richmond, Jeffrey Morse, with whom she has been working for about five years, but only this past year on pair driving. She bought the second Morgan horse, Galen, from Jeff, who has helped her with pair driving and in relaxing her tense Morgan gelding, Max. Jeff has been breeding Morgans and training horses in Richmond since 1974 and conducts driving clinics throughout the country. Lyn says that Jeff is a "solution finder."

When I asked Lyn how she feels about the dangers of driving, whether small carts or larger carriages, she confirmed that she is fully aware that driving has its special dangers. She related a few instances of accidents, but they are clearly not her focus.

Part of the pleasure for carriage drivers is the sociability, and Lyn is no exception. She is active in her local Saratoga Driving Association, the Green Mountain Horse Association, and the Colonial Carriage and Driving Society. After my interview with her over lunch in Shelburne Falls, she suggested that I accompany her on her prearranged visit to the home of nearby carriage drivers, where perhaps—if the rain stopped—I would have the opportunity to be a passenger on a carriage drive. She was eager to discuss and learn about hitching a pair and the pros and cons of a yoke versus crab attachment to the pole. Of course, I was delighted at the opportunity.

So off we went to visit Peter and Gioia Bravmann, who are known as expert drivers. Peter generally drives a pair of large Gelderlanders, a handsome European combination of warmblood and draft. The Bravmanns own acres and acres of forested land with drivable roads running throughout. These carriage roads were built by Peter and Gioia themselves. Ten horses are stabled in a well-set-up barn. Nearby is a tremendous, naturally lighted, indoor arena, although Peter said it really is not large enough to drive a pair within it. They do have some stable help, but Peter and Gioia regularly care for, groom, and exercise their horses themselves, particularly in preparation for upcoming events. Carriage driving is their life—this is what they do, and they do it splendidly and successfully.

After some carriage-driving talk inside their home, this couple graciously harnessed and hooked the two Gelderlanders for a drive. Lyn had told me that preparing a pair for a drive can take up to an hour. Under the circumstances, with the rain perhaps only temporarily stopped and several people working at the job, not that much time elapsed before the two horses were hitched to the carriage and off we went for a delightful hour's drive. Lyn was up front discussing driving techniques with Peter while I was in back with Gioia and a drive-loving dog. What a treat.

Need I say that I did not question Lyn about when and how she planned to stop riding and driving? She is on an upswing, not a downswing, having started on a new and exciting adventure with pair driving. Quitting is far from her mind.

*Nona King at 44 jumping Budget Bound at a New York horse show*

# NONA KING

## Age 78
## New Salem

Nona must love horses very much indeed for her to have
consented to an interview with me on March 1, and then to
have warmly welcomed me into her house to discuss her life
with horses. I say her house, not her home, because the home
she and her husband owned in New Salem suffered a serious
fire this past December. At the time of my interview, they were
living in the house of next-door neighbors who are spending the
winter in Florida.

More importantly, just this January, Nona lost her oldest son,
Gary Pond, to lung cancer. Add to all this the fact that Lille, a
black Labrador Retriever, had just presented Nona with a litter
of nine puppies. Meanwhile, the insurance company needed
all sorts of information about what was lost in the fire, most
of which must be found and retrieved from their burned-out
house and presented in appropriate form—not next month, but
tomorrow, of course. And yet Nona was generously able to settle
down with me for three hours to speak about horses and dogs.

First came the dogs. As I entered, I heard a low growl from
a very serious Lille who was not about to let a stranger hurt
her pups. Nona assured me that Lille would not attack, so I
boldly walked right by the dog, not even glancing at her to
make eye contact. (I was obeying the advice of TV's popular
Dog Whisperer.) I did, however, turn my eyes to the adorable
bundle of wiggling blackness in a box in the far corner of the
livingroom. How could I not? This litter is the sixty-fourth
that Nona has bred. And Lille is not her only dog, the others
being cared for temporarily by her daughter. For years Nona has
been deeply into the Laborador Retriever business, with all that
entails in the way of daily care, showing, and travel.

Nona knew from the start that she would make working with animals her career. She took a pre-veterinary course at Cornell University, graduating in 1953 with a major in animal husbandry. She had not been accepted in the veterinary course because she was a woman! Nona was on the equestrian team in college and played polo although again, as a woman in the early fifties, she was not allowed to play in competitions. She married another Cornell University graduate soon after, then came military service years, and the first four of six children. She lived on her first husband's dairy farm, where the Yale polo ponies were summered.

After her husband completed service with the U.S. Air Force, the family moved back to the Connecticut dairy farm, where sport parachuting had started. Soon after, Parachutes, Inc., opened the first U.S. commercial parachuting school in Orange, and the '62 International Sport Parachuting competition was held in the U.S. for the first time. Nona was on a three-woman jump team at the event.

During this exciting period, Nona had not forgotten horses. In 1957, she acquired her first horse, a gray Thoroughbred mare, sired by a Yale polo pony and named Budget Bound. She showed her at Eastern State in hunter class, where she did well, and also in the New England pleasure class, where she won second in a field of thirty Morgan contestants. Budget Bound was a very difficult loader, so to get her on a trailer Nona discovered that a bit of beer—yes, beer—offered in the hand would do the trick. Nona noted that "this was before the horse whisperer philosophy had developed." Budget Bound was bred for the first and only time at age eighteen and foaled a lovely steel-gray filly. Nona regretted having to sell her as a green three-year-old, but family commitments, including six children, were overwhelming.

Nona told me about an amusing incident that occurred at the Eastern State competition. She had trailered her horse down alone and was doing the cleanup, grooming, and such in the stall assigned to her horse. By the second day, a guy working in the stall next door to her asked her when her "man" was coming. Nona thought he meant her husband, but after a moment's confusion realized that he meant her groom for the horses. Apparently, at that time and in that place, a woman handling her horse completely by herself at a big competition was unusual.

Later on, Nona used her animal husbandry education by working for fifteen years with the veterinarians at what is now the Adams Animal Hospital, starting when Walter Jaworski owned the practice. She not only handled front desk work, but with her previous animal experience, was able to be helpful in examining the animals. For a brief time, in fact, she accompanied the veterinarian on farm calls when that was part of the practice.

Nona occasionally has participated in competitive trail rides, mentioning one in Barre, but I gather that her primary interest has been in showing and trail riding. Briefly, she and her daughter Tara tried dressage, but neither became enamored of the discipline.

Meanwhile, Nona had seen and acquired Red, a four-year-old chestnut Quarter Horse gelding, at Franklin Turkey Farm in Gill. Finding herself in the midst of bantam chickens, Nona decided to bring a boxful home with her, thinking that it would accustom her gray mare and her daughter's large hunter pony to farm animals they might meet on the trail. She and her daughter had a wonderful period of trail riding together.

When she mentioned crossing Route 202 and riding in the Quabbin, I of course raised my eyebrows, remarking that I thought riding in the Quabbin was strictly prohibited. Nona grinned, admitting that it was and that she had some fun evading the men patrolling the area, who obviously must have seen hoofprints but did not bother to find her. (I myself have never put horse hoof inside the Quabbin, but I happen to know that there are still a few hoofprints to be found there on occasion. It is such a tempting place for all of us trail riding people in the area!)

Finally in 1980, while Nona was with her Labradors at the Virginia Specialty Show, her trusty gray mare, Budget Bound, became critically sick and had to be put down on her return. The gelding Red and the mare had become close friends, with Red neighing, whimpering, and running around unhappily whenever the mare was ridden out without him. Nona recounts her surprise at how differently Red acted when the gray mare was led out to be put down. No neighing and carrying on. He just stood there and watched her being led off. Nona is sure that somehow Red knew and accepted.

Red himself was not the safest of mounts, having a way of suddenly dipping a shoulder in such a fashion that, if the rider wasn't paying attention, she would be thrown forward and off. Then there was briefly a free Thoroughbred mare named Sara with only one eye, apparently having run into a tree in a pasture at some time. She had been in a hunter show barn, so knew her way around the show ring adequately but could not show in hunter classes any longer because of the missing eye.

Nona's present horse, visible from the neighbors' house in his barn and pasture, is Mike, formally Hot Order, a 16-hand Thoroughbred bay gelding. Nona bought him when he was five in May 1995. With occasional help from local trainer Stephanie Baer, Nona has trained him, working toward hunting classes and eventing. "He can buck," says Nona. In fact, at one point recently while Stephanie was riding him, he showed extreme discomfort and nearly dumped her. It was obvious that the gelding was in pain, so Nona called in veterinarian Robert Schmitt as well as Mary Kahan, who does chiropractic and acupuncture work. The general diagnosis was sacrum problems, which have worsened.

Meanwhile, Nona herself has been far from free of physical problems. To mention just a few, she broke her wrist when all four feet of her horse splayed beneath her and she fell under him. For someone taking care of horses and dogs, that is not only a major injury but a great inconvenience. Her knees have given her trouble, and she had to have a hip replacement in 2004. During this time, Stephanie was training Mike because Nona could not ride after the surgery. In fact, her last time on a horse was before her hip replacement in 2004.

*Nona with Mike in 1998*

So what about the future? Dr. Schmitt has told her that Mike is "an accident waiting to happen," and her own doctor has warned her about the risk of dislocating her second hip if she were to take another fall. As an experienced horsewoman, Nona knows that even the best of riders can be dumped, including herself. Mike cannot be ridden now or possibly ever. To get back into riding, she would have to acquire another horse and begin training all over again. This is more than she can think about at the moment—understandably, particularly considering recent events in her life.

Meanwhile, she says that of course Mike will remain with her to live out his life. "I cannot imagine starting the day without going to the barn," she said. She herself does all the feeding and stall work, although her husband usually cleans the pasture. She not only attends her horse the usual three times a day but also goes out about 11 PM to give just a bit more hay, water, and carrots for overnight. Although chores sometimes have become more uncomfortable, especially in zero-degree weather, she says "horse and dog activities *are* my life."

When I asked about her future with horses and riding, Nona paused. Then she said that she just doesn't know what the future will hold and that ofttimes we don't have to rush to make decisions. Things are likely to work out for the best in their own time. As someone who tends to force herself to make decisions, I listened with particular and personal interest. I could tell from Nona's body language that she was not just repeating a happy sentiment she had heard from others. She was expressing something she herself has found to be true. This is the wisdom that sometimes comes from living a while.

*Don Roberts at 74 setting out on Jessie*

# DON ROBERTS

## Age 75
## Gilbertville

Here is the quintessential New England COWBOY, capital letters. Don Roberts, at seventy-five, is out there riding Western-style despite a back that keeps telling him it's time to stop. When I put the question to him about quitting, he simply said, "Nope, never think about it."

What Don *does* think about are his horses and the next chance to ride, either with a special group from Ware (all considerably younger, of course), with individual friends, or best of all, out at a ranch in Wyoming where he goes for two weeks at a time to help out with special jobs. Here at home he manages to ride about twice a week, weather permitting.

Don's first acquaintance with horses was at his grandfather's farm. There were eighteen horses, but he remembers in particular a Quarter Horse mare that he would ride in his early teens. He also tells about an off-the-track trotter named Melissa Day that was used to rake hay—the old-fashioned way, with a dump rake. Young Don was behind this horse when they raked up a yellow jacket nest. Before he could dump the hay, the yellow jackets were all over both him and the horse. Melissa Day, of course, just took off, heading for the barn. Now the barn was one that had a large door at each end. As the horse started through the door with the rake behind him, the rake, which was wider than the door opening, hit the barn at full tilt. The harness broke, the horse kept going, and Don landed half way down the barn. Remembering, Don remarked, "That was sure some ride."

Don grew up in Lexington, where in the early fifties the president of the Foxboro Raceway had a training stable and horse track. Don gravitated to the track and soon made friends with the trainers, who gave him a job cleaning stalls and tack. As his friendship with the trainers grew, it became apparent that he had a great interest in horses. They soon asked him if he would like to start driving. However, after finding himself behind a few runaway horses, he decided that driving was not for him. He grins as he calls it "too dangerous." The grin, of course, is because most riders would find some of Don's own mounts too dangerous, as he well knows.

Leaving Lexington for the Hardwick area in 1963, he became joint owner of Hanson and Roberts, LLC, where he and his partner ran a dairy farm with 130-140 dairy cows and also sold hay. The knowledge that he gained about the most effective feed for his cows and also the ingredients of various types of hay and grain has been useful as he has transferred it to keeping his horses fit. He has strong convictions on the proper way to feed horses.

As if running a dairy farm and producing mountains of hay a year were not demanding enough, Don became Hardwick's police chief at the age of forty-two. When he retired twenty years later, his retirement gift from the town was a trip to a Wyoming ranch with his wife, and there began the many excursions over the years to the ranch where he still visits to help out and ride whatever horse they give him for the job he has to do.

Over the years, he has ridden and owned many horses, but at present he lives with his wife Paula in a small house on 285 acres with two horses. One is Major, a quiet black Tennessee Walker gelding about ten years old that he has owned for only a few years. This is one of those wonderful horses that anyone can ride, Don says. And then there is the other, clearly his favorite, by the name of Jesse. She is a stunningly beautiful chestnut Quarter Horse mare rescued out of a killer pen—and that tells you something right off. Don just fell in love with her, plain and simple, despite her delight in bucking that landed her in the killer pen to begin with. She is about nineteen years old and, simply, "hot." Which is clearly the type of horse that Don enjoys.

Don is one of those people who continues to learn. At present, he is experimenting with the theories and equipment of Horse Tenders, a group that recommends and sells a particular kind of bitless bridle. Don showed one to me and explained how it worked on the lower jaw of the horse. He uses the bitless bridle on both horses. Another modern trend that Don has embraced for his horses is keeping them barefoot, and to this end he has learned how to do his own trimming. That sounds hard on his back, but he does it anyway.

Although safety is not Don's favorite subject, I inquired about what he does to increase his own safety when mounted, observing that of course he wears a helmet, but what else does he do? I was shocked to hear him say that he never wears a helmet. And why not, said I. "Cowboys do not wear helmets" was the reply. I really laughed at that and exchanged glances with his wife, who was nearby at that moment. We accused him of pride, which he laughingly admitted. It comes down to the fact that Don is both supremely confident and also enjoys his image as a cowboy. Boys will be boys.

I ought to add here that he does "strongly advise young people and others who don't have total confidence in their horse to wear one." He also had a few words about people who acquire horses who may be beautiful but are beyond their ability to control, noting the danger of an out-of-control trail horse both to the rider and also to the people riding with them.

Continuing on the safety topic, I learned that his wife, Paula, a sometime rider but not a horse person, had been seriously injured in the mid 1990s on a new horse that had seemed, but obviously was not, safe. The injury required weeks in the hospital. Sensibly, she then stopped riding.

I broadened the safety topic to include the issue of comfort. Don rides in an Australian stock saddle developed by Clint Anderson. He explained how the saddle provides ways to stay aboard when a horse starts to buck and that the saddle is very comfortable for him despite the four bone spurs in his back. He smilingly noted that using this style of Australian saddle is "more like a cowboy." For added comfort, he always wears a back support beneath his outer clothing and a back magnet as well. He pointed out that the sofa on which he was sitting had a magnet pad on it, which he finds helpful.

I expect that Don will never finally dismount but will eventually ride off into the sunset, still a cowboy. Nevertheless,

*Don at 75 shoeing Jessie*

my visit with him must have stirred up some thoughts and feelings, because a few weeks afterward he wrote this poem and sent it to me.

## The One Last Ride

As the old rider left his house, he looked to the sky with a smile on his face and a tear in his eye. He said to himself, what a great day for this one last ride.

As he walked to the barn with many thoughts on his mind, he heard his favorite mare give a whinny, for she also knew that this day would be their one last ride.

He brushed and groomed her with great pride. Then tack was set in place and checked over twice, because he knew this would be their one last ride.

As they rode down the trail, many thoughts came to him of the great horse he rode, the friends he had made, and he hoped they would understand that this would be his one last ride.

So as the trail was coming to an end, he wants to thank his wife and friends for letting him have this one last great ride.

I think Don's poem is an appropriate, although sad, ending to our celebration of elder riders. He writes of a moment we all fear but one that I suspect is rare. No longer riding is indeed, as I phrased it earlier, a haunting eventuality, but the actual decision to quit may be made for some of us by the vagaries of living, by situations not under our control. Regardless of how our own last ride happens, we will have to hope that by then we have the wisdom to accept our aging, to adapt to circumstances we may not like, and to appreciate how horses have enriched our lives—and will continue to do so in our remembrance of them.

# Afterword

At the end of some of the preceding sketches, I am sure the reader must be asking a question or two about what has happened since the interview. I have certainly wondered myself. Because twelve of the interviews were written during the fall of 2009, quite a time ago, I decided to contact a few of these people and ask the particular question about each that has been in my mind. Below are the results of this follow-up.

Donald Grypko is still looking for his perfect horse. He says he found a fine buckskin at a camp, but the horse is not for sale right now because all the kids love him. Donald will try again for that horse in the fall and meanwhile keep on looking.

Beth Jenkins is once again Show Manager for the New England Dressage Association's (NEDA's) Fall Festival of Dressage from September 14 to 19, 2010. The June 2010 issue of *Horsemen's Yankee Pedlar*, in an article on NEDA, noted that the organization this year celebrates its fiftieth anniversary, with Beth a member from the start.

Pat Kane has not yet found her ideal horse, and in fact told me that she plans to move to Florida permanently this summer, where she says she will continue her search.

Nona King now lives in a forty-five-foot trailer, on the same property but slightly east of her former house, which is in the final stages of demolition. She and her husband have finalized plans for building a new house almost on the site of the previous one, which was several hundred years old. She says she is working on her garden, which remains in place, and her horse, Mike, is still with her. She added, unasked, that she misses riding.

Judy Smith has not bought another horse, nor did she lease one this summer. However, she has been riding with a friend in Ashby who has more than one horse. And she has promised to come ride my second horse with me in the fall.

Whitey Streeter turned ninety years old toward the end of June, and his daughter organized a well-attended celebration for him at a fine local restaurant. Meanwhile, not long before, he was on patrol as Bernardston dog officer in the car with Police Chief Jim Palmeri at the time he arrested at gunpoint the suspected murderer of four people. Palmeri gave Whitey credit for spotting the suspect's vehicle after they had temporarily lost sight of it around a curve. Whitey retired as dog officer on June 30, 2010. He died on August 27, 2010.

# After Afterword

A year has passed since I began this book in September 2009 and started to find and interview twenty other elder riders. As I completed the manuscript, I began to hear my "gentle reader," that valued intimate of so many writers before me, asking, "Well, Helen, what have you learned that will help you personally? You set out to discover the pros and cons, the whys and wherefores, the hows and whethers about riding beyond the age of seventy from riders facing similar aging issues. What did you learn from your quest? Have you decided if you yourself will continue riding beyond eighty?"

The quick, as well as truthful, answer is: "No, not really. Not yet." Discussion of the topic has been helpful in deepening and broadening my consideration of what I myself should do. I started out quite certain that my riding would continue in spring and autumn in much the same way as before. And I did ride all last fall as usual, up until hunting season began in early December.

But then it happened. The unexpected. My primary riding buddy, Jean (considerably younger than I), had an odd, not-horse-related, accident in mid-December that still prevents her from riding often. She and her sixty-four-pound hunting dog ran into each other, and the miniscus and the medial collateral ligament in her right knee were torn. (The dog was just fine.) Even after months of rest and continuing therapy, ensuing pain in her hips makes mounting and riding very uncomfortable. She continues to drive horses with a friend, but riding trails with me regularly in the near future is clearly out of the question.

As discussed above, in order to maintain confidence and enjoy the sport, it is necessary to ride regularly. Regular riding for me has four major requirements. The first is general health plus strong, relatively pain-free knees, hips, and back; the second is two sound, easy-going horses; the third is a regular riding buddy or two; and finally, easily accessible and familiar trails. I have the first and the second, not presently the third. As for the fourth, many of the trees in what I consider "my" hour-long trail are being harvested. That means blocked trails and scary noises from big machines and falling trees. Oh my.

Let's just say that I am working on the situation and waiting to see what develops. I am remembering Nona King's wise comment that we don't have to rush to make decisions, that things are apt to work out for the best in their own time. And of course there are various other back-up options as discussed above.

Meanwhile, I am thoroughly enjoying caring for my amiable horses morning, noon, and night. This past summer, when in the evening I would open the gate to the far pasture for them to go out and graze all night, they would each stand quietly near the gate while I adjusted a fly coat or fly mask, or perhaps just patted a neck or flank. Then they would move on out. I experienced a wave of love for them each evening. Such waves are invaluable— the stuff of happiness.

And recently a brilliant idea popped into my head as to how I could enjoy my horses even more, an idea that will benefit me as long as horses remain in my pastures. The idea was to remove a high and long row of bushes between the house and the pastures that heretofore had blocked most of the view of my horses. I immediately had these bushes removed. Now I can sit at the kitchen table or walk to the window of the sunroom and see what my Lucky and Lulu are up to. I find considerable pleasure in this. It quiets me. And as necessary, it also comforts me.

I ask myself why I didn't think of this idea years ago. Never mind. I have thought of it now, the bushes have been removed. The timing of the idea was perhaps just right. As also was the timing of this book, beginning as it does with my remembrances of two little slices of heaven. They will last, no matter what else happens.

# Glossary of Equestrian Terms

**Classes:** Horse shows are divided into classes, varying with discipline, age of rider, and experience level. Those mentioned in this book include halter class, where the rider is not mounted, but leads her horse, which is wearing a halter rather than a bridle; reining class, for Western riders to show their abilities in using their reins to control a horse's speed and direction; and trail class, where horse and rider are judged on their ability to quietly negotiate simulated challenging objects that might be met on a trail, such as a bridge crossing or a mailbox.

**Cushing's disease:** A disease caused when the cortex of the adrenal gland produces excessive amounts of hormones, including cortisol. The signs include long hair, thin skin, fragile bones, stupor, weakness and sweating. (This definition is the one given by *Equus* in the Spring 2006 issue.)

**Dressage:** A riding discipline in which the rider guides the horse into various maneuvers of gait and pace with barely perceptible movement of hands, legs, and weight.

**Equitation:** A riding class in horse shows that includes walking, trotting, and cantering, but not jumping. Judges award a rider's skill, not a horse's natural ability.

**Gaited:** Refers to a horse that by breeding takes naturally to gaits other than the walk, trot, canter, and gallop. These gaits are usually in speed somewhere between a walk and a trot and are notably smoother for the rider than the trot. Gaits are distinguished by the rhythm and order in which a horse's feet hit the ground. (In a trot, a horse's left front and right back hit the ground at the same time, as do the right front and left back.) Gaited horses include the Fox Trotter, the Paso Fino, and the Tennessee Walking Horse.

**Gelding:** A male horse that has been castrated, or gelded.

**Green and green-broke:** A green horse is one who has probably never been ridden and never trained to understand and respond to the rider's signals. A green-broke horse has been taught the basics and sometimes responds properly, but cannot be relied upon.

**Gymkhana activities:** Horseback-riding activities featuring games and novelty contests.

**Hand:** Four inches. A horse's height is measured in terms of hands. It is the distance from the ground to the horse's withers (the large bone at the front of the back just before the neck). A number after the period indicates another inch. For example, 15.2 hands equals 62 inches.

**Longe:** To guide, train, or exercise a horse using a long rein or strap, usually in a circle around the trainer.

**Off the track:** Refers to a horse that has been trained to race, either in pacing and trotting races or in Thoroughbred running races. A horse who is off the track usually is an excitable animal, has little or no experience on trails, and requires retraining for riding in arenas and on trails.

**Post:** To adjust to a horse's trot by rising up and down in the saddle. Posting is done primarily but not exclusively by English-style riders.

**Pulls and jigs:** A horse that pulls is not responding to the rider's shortening of the reins to request a slowing down and thus is pulling against the rider. A horse that jigs does a short, bouncy trot instead of a walk when asked to slow down. Often a horse will do both at the same time, usually when excited or approaching his own barn.

**Shy:** A quick sideways movement by a horse that is frightened or alarmed.

**Snaffle bit:** A mild bit. There are many varieties of snaffle, but the key feature is that the rings connecting the bit to the reins are on each side of the mouth rather than beneath it. It guides the horse by direct pressure and is used mostly but not exclusively by English-style riders.

**Turnback:** The rider in Western cattle herding competitions responsible for turning back cattle straying from the herd.

*Helen Hills*

## About the Author

Helen Hills was born in Reading, Pennsylvania, graduated with honors from Wellesley College, and raised four children in the Washington, D.C. area. After working as a writer for the U.S. Department of Education for twenty-five years, she moved to the village of Warwick, Massachusetts, where she lives with her husband, two horses, and two dogs. She has been working with elders as a volunteer for nineteen years. And she is "still riding at eighty."

Text and captions for *Still Riding at 80* are set in Adobe Garamond Premier Pro, which had its genesis in 1988 when Adobe senior type designer Robert Slimbach visited the Plantin-Moretus Museum in Antwerp, Belgium, to study their collection of Claude Garamond's metal punches and type designs. Garamond, a French punchcutter, produced a refined array of book types in the mid-1500s that combined an unprecedented degree of balance and elegance, and stand as a pinnacle of beauty and practicality in typefounding. While fine-tuning Adobe Garamond (released in 1989) as a useful design suited to modern publishing, Slimbach started planning an entirely new interpretation of Garamond's designs based on the large range of unique sizes he had seen at the Plantin-Moretus, and on the comparable italics cut by Robert Granjon, Garamond's contemporary. By modeling Garamond Premier Pro on these hand-cut type sizes, Slimbach has retained the varied optical size characteristics and freshness of the original designs, while creating a practical 21st-century type family. Garamond Premier Pro contains an extensive glyph complement, including central European, Cyrillic and Greek characters, and is offered in five weights ranging from light to bold.

Titles and subtitles are set in Kabel, designed by Rudolf Koch and released in 1927 by the Klingspor foundry in Germany. Kabel is named in honor of the laying of the first trans-Atlantic telephone cable. Kabel was one of the first geometric sans serif designs directly influenced by the Bauhaus movement. Kabel's geometric proportions are integrated with humanistic features, resulting in a sans serif typeface that is functional in text and elegant in display work.